How to Cho Automate Your Aquaponic/Hydroponic Garden with Arduino/Genuino

by

David Leithauser

Copyright © 2017 David Leithauser

All Rights Reserved

Table of Contents

- Introduction 3
- Getting Started with Arduino 6
- A Simple Timer 23
- Air Temperature and Humidity 40
- Water Temperature 59
- Water Level 64
- Moisture Levels in Soil 87
- Testing and Controlling pH 101
- Electrical conductivity (total dissolved solids) 140
- Turbidity 194
- Displaying data on screen 201
- Displaying Data on a Web page 209
- More Ideas and Information 224

Introduction

Arduinos are small computers on a circuit board. (Note: Outside the US, Arduinos are called Genuinos.) Unlike computers that have a keyboard, mouse, and display and are designed to input and output information, Arduinos are designed to observe and control physical objects. You can connect sensors to the Arduino inputs and relays or other devices to the outputs. You can then program the Arduino to perform various output actions based on the input. Arduinos are used as controller circuits for a wide range of devices.

In this book, I explain ways that you can use one or more Arduinos to monitor or automate your aquaponic or hydroponic garden. By monitor, I mean using it as a test instrument to report on conditions like water level, water and air temperature, pH, total dissolved solids, turbidity (cloudiness), etc. It is possible to sound alarms based on this information, display this information directly on a small screen connected to the Arduino, or even display information on a Web page. By automate, I mean actually act on the information directly. For example, it can monitor water levels and raise or lower water levels as necessary, monitor air or water temperature and turn on heaters or cooling systems, pump the water through a filter if it gets too cloudy, add chemicals to correct imbalances, and so on.

There are several advantages to building your own control systems using Arduinos. One is that it can often be cheaper, especially if one Arduino is doing a dozen different things, replacing several off-the-shelf devices. More importantly, Arduinos can be more flexible than off-the-shelf products. For example, if you use an Arduino as a timer, you can control exactly how long you want things to be on and off, down to the second (actually, millisecond, but let's not get silly here). You can also have it turn one (or more) thing on when it turns another off. Most importantly, you can integrate many of your operations. For example, you can program it to perform an operation, like pumping water, if the water is above a certain level and the temperature is above a certain point and the pump has been off for at least a certain amount of time, and so on. That is, you can have a smart aquaponic or hydroponic farm.

In this book, I dedicate the first chapter to a description of the very basics of Arduinos for those readers that are totally unfamiliar with them. I will describe what they are, how the set up the basic hardware and software you will need to use them, even where to buy them. In each of the following chapters, I will show you how to perform a specific task with the Arduino, like creating timers for flooding and draining your systems that adjust themselves for temperature and humidity, monitoring pH and automatically adding chemicals to balance it when necessary, and so on. I will provide you with specific, usable code that you can load into the Arduino, and show you how to modify this code to make any adjustments you might need to match it to your system. If you are familiar with Arduinos, you will probably be able to greatly expand in the code I give you to develop very sophisticated systems. If you are not familiar with Arduinos, you will be able to simply install and use the code as-is, changing just a few numbers in the code as I will explain to make it fit your system.

Note: This book is not intended to be a book an introductory or comprehensive book of aquaponics or hydroponics. This book is intended for people who are already familiar with one or both of those subjects and probably are already at least started on building these systems, if not already using them. I will therefore not get into great detail discussing the basics of aquaponics or hydroponics. I will, for example, not get into detailed discussions of pumping systems or other components of aquaponics/hydroponics. I will not get very heavily into discussions of wiring safety or other aspects of connecting your heavy equipment, although I will touch on these as they relate directly to connecting things to the Arduinos. The purpose of this book is to show you how to make your system run more efficiently by using Arduinos to automate your system so that it responds quickly and effectively to any conditions that might kill your fish or plants or damage your equipment. It will also show you how to monitor your system more easily. In addition to showing you how to make your system run more efficiently, this book can also save you money by showing you how to equip your system more cheaply, since profession aquaponic or hydroponic equipment can run into the thousands of dollars. While this book assumes you are familiar with aquaponics or hydroponics, it does not assume that you are expert or even familiar with Arduinos. I will provide enough information for even those readers totally unfamiliar with Arduinos to apply the techniques in this book to your systems.

Notice: The designs in this book are intended to help you monitor and maintain your aquaponic or hydroponic systems. However, devices like the designs in this book are not infallible. Any electronic devices, especially delicate equipment like some of the projects in this book, are subject to malfunctions, deterioration, errors, and similar problems. The devices in this book should be considered an addition or assistance to your normal procedures for maintaining your system, and should not replace normal testing and maintenance of your system. In addition, I cannot guarantee the applicability of any particular design to your particular system. By using the information in this book, you agree that the author and publisher of this book are not responsible for any damage or loss to your system (e.g., fish, plants, equipment, etc.) caused by use, misuse, or overdependence on the instruments and ideas described in this book.

Chapter 1

Getting Started with Arduino

This chapter will explain the very basics of buying, wiring, and programming Arduinos. Note that this chapter is not intended to be a detailed or comprehensive course in Arduino hardware or programming. There are many books you can buy on these subjects if you want to, such as "Arduino: a comprehensive starting up guide for complete beginners", "Arduino for Dummies", "Arduino Programming for Beginners in Projects and Examples: How to Get Started", and many other books. You will also find the Web site Arduino.cc a useful reference source. The purpose of this chapter is to provide enough basic information for people who are totally unfamiliar with Arduinos to buy Arduinos, connect things to them, and install the code in this book on Arduinos. You can skip this chapter if you are already familiar with Arduinos. However, there are a few tips that even most experienced Arduinos users might not know, so it might be a good idea to go ahead and read this chapter anyway.

Describing Arduinos can get a bit complicated, because Arduinos are open source. This means that the inventors did not try to patent it and keep it to themselves. Instead, they released the plans and invited everyone to manufacturer them. They also encourage everyone to improve on the Arduinos and come up with new types and new features. This has resulted in many different models of Arduinos with many different features. For example, there are Arduinos with built-in Wi-Fi chips, like the MKR1000 and the WeMos D1 R2. There are Arduinos with different numbers of input and output connections. There are also many manufacturers of most models, resulting in many makes with slight differences in such features as how much current they can supply. In this chapter, I will discuss two of the most common models, the Arduino Uno and the Arduino Mega. Figures 1.1 and 1.2 show the Uno and the Mega, respectively. The Uno shown is a particular make called the Buono, which has a few features I like.

Figure 1.1

Figure 1.2

These Arduinos have female connectors (holes where you can insert wires) in rows called heads to connect the Arduino with other devices. These connections are called pins, even though they are actually holes. There are analog and digital connections. The Uno has 6 analog connections, labeled A0 to A5. The Mega has 16, labeled A0 to A15. (Note: On the Mega shown, the A is missing on analog pin 6 because a mounting hole does not leave space for it.) You can apply a voltage from 0 to 5 volts DC to these inputs. The Arduino will normally convert this voltage internally to a number from 0 to 1023, although some models allow you to change this to 0 to 4095 for higher resolution.

There are also digital connections that can be either input or output. You tell the Arduino whether each of these is an input or output in the code when you program it, as will be explained later. The Uno/Buono has 14 of these, labeled 0 to 13. The Mega has 54 of these, numbered 0 to 53. If you set a digital connection as an input, you apply a voltage of either 0 volts or 5 volts to the connection, indicating off/on. If it is set for output, it will output a voltage of either 0 or 5 volts. This can be used to turn something on or off, or can be used to provide more complicated information when combined together. Some of the digital connections are capable of Pulse Width Modulation (PWM), which means that they are not just on or off. They can be made to output a square wave with a frequency of about 500 Hz that you can control the percentage of the time the output is on and off. You can tell it, for example, to be on for 60% of the time and off for 40%. You can use this to control the power going to a device. For example, you can control the brightness of a light or the speed of a motor. These are marked with a # on the Uno and labeled PWM on the Mega (2 through 13). You can also see that some are labeled TX or RX. This means that these can also be used for serial communication.

There are additional connections. The ones labeled GND are ground connections, which is the same as - on a battery. Most devices connected to a digital output will also be connected to this, unless you want a 0 output to indicate on. There are also connections labeled 5V and 3V3 or 3.3V. These supply power of 5 volts DC and 3.3 volts DC respectively. The connection labeled VIN supplies positive voltage that depends on how you are powering the Arduino. It is usually about 1 volt less than your power supply. It can also be used to power the Arduino if you connect a power supply like a battery to it. However, both of these are tricky and can cause damage to either the Arduino or the device connected to it unless done correctly, so I advise against using this pin unless you are very familiar with Arduinos and electronics in general. The connection labeled reset will reset your Arduino if you connect it to ground (GND), causing the program running on the Arduino to start over at the beginning. You would not normally want to do this, unless the Arduino seems to be malfunctioning. There is also a reset button on the Arduino that has the same effect. The AREF and IOREF connections are designed to allow you to change the levels of analog and digital input and output, respectively. They are used only in specialized situations that will not come up in this book.

Connecting to the Arduino

You can connect to these input/outputs several ways. A 22 to 24-gauge single core wire will fit. You can also use cables generally called Dupont connector cables. These come in ribbons as shown in Figure 1.3. They can easily be pulled apart for individual cables.

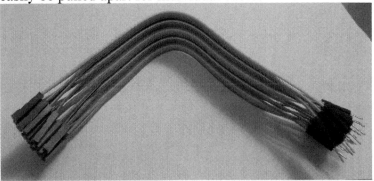

Figure 1.3

There are three varieties of these cables: male-male, male-female, and female-female, indicating the type of connectors on the end. The one shown in Figure 1.3 is male-female, indicating that it has a male connector on one end and a female connector on the other end. When ordering these cables for the Arduino, you would want the male connector on at least one end to fit into the holes on the Arduino connector. The type of connector you want on the other end depends on whether the device you are connecting it to has a male or female connector. These also come in various lengths, usually 20 to 40 cm.

Although Dupont cables or 22-gauge wire are convenient for connecting to your Arduino, they do have the disadvantage that your project is not very sturdy in the long run. The wires are not held in securely, and can come loose. For final projects, it is best to use a screw shield. (Devices that fit onto the top of the Arduino are called shields because they look like a shield on top the Arduino.) A screw shield is a board that fits firmly onto the top of the Arduino and provides tight connections to wires. A typical screw shield is shown in Figure 1.4.

Figure 1.4

This has pins on the bottom that fit directly into the female connectors on the Arduino Uno, Mega, and other models. (Note that it only connects to the Uno connections, so when used with a Mega you will need to use other methods to connect to the remaining connections.) On the sides are holes where you insert a wire and clamps to grip the wire. At the top are screws that you rotate counter-clockwise to open the clamps and then rotate clockwise to close the clamps so they grip the wire. Figure 1.5 shows the shield from the side.

Figure 1.5

These screw shields also have the advantage of providing you with holes at the top where you can mount components such as resistors that are part of your circuits.

Powering the Arduino

There are several ways to power the Arduino. One way is with a USB cable. In Figures 1.1 and 1.2, at the top right you can see a USB connector port. The type of connector varies with the different makes and models of the Arduino. When purchasing an Arduino, try to buy one that comes with its own USB cable if possible to make sure that you have one that fits the Arduino connector. Just plug the cable into the Arduino port and the other end of the cable into any USB port. Most likely, you will want it to be a USB port that plugs into a wall, such as the ones in Figure 1.7.

Figure 1.7

If you want portability, you can power it using the type of power bank portable charger that you can use to charge your phone on the go, as shown in Figure 1.8.

Figure 1.8

These are charged up by plugging them into a USB port power supply such as the one in Figure 1.7. You can then draw power from them by plugging your USB powered device, such as your Arduino, into the power bank. It is important to note that some of these power banks allow you to draw power from them while they are plugged in and charging, and some do not. That is, some turn off the output power while they are charging. You definitely want to use one that will provide power while it is charging. This will allow you to plug the Arduino into the power bank and the power bank into the USB power plug. The Arduino can run off the power bank, and the power bank will not discharge because it is constantly being recharged. Thus, the power bank acts as an uninterruptible power supply for your Arduino. Any power interruptions will not shut down the Arduino or cause it to reset.

Another way to power the Arduino is with the DC barrel jack shown in the upper left corner of the Arduinos shown in Figures 1.1 and 1.2. These can accept a DC voltage from either a battery or wall plug, and shown in Figure 1.9.

Figure 1.9

The one on the left plugs into the wall, and the one on the right runs off a 9-volt battery. The allowable volts that you can apply to the DC barrel jack varies with the make and model of the Arduino you use. For the standard Arduino, the range is 7 to 12 volts. For the BUONO, it is 6 to 24. This is one of the reasons I prefer the BUONO. This is especially important if you want to run it off 4 batteries such as AAA or D cells, since this will provide 6 volts. It is also important if you are running it off a car battery, since these can exceed 12 volts. One interesting thing to be aware of is that if you are providing power to both the USB port and the DC barrel jack at more than about 6.6 volts, the Arduino will accept the power from the DC barrel jack and not use the power from the USB port. Thus, you could power the Arduino off a wall plug as shown in Figure 1.9 and have the USB port connected to a power bank as shown in Figure 1.8 as a backup power supply in case of power failure.

There is another option for powering the Arduino. You can connect the negative terminal of a battery to the GND (ground) input of the Arduino and the positive battery terminal to the Arduino VIN connector. This is almost the same as connecting the battery to the DC barrel jack, with two differences. First, this can power the Arduino with a slightly lower voltage than using the DC barrel jack, which is useful if you are using a power supply that just marginally supplies the necessary voltage, like 4 D cells.

Second, the VIN connection does not provide reverse polarity protection like the DC barrel jack does. This means that if you accidentally reverse the positive and negative on the battery when you connect it, you will fry your Arduino. Thus, powering the Arduino by the VIN connection is generally not a good idea, although I have done it on some projects. It is probably hypothetical in projects where you are using the Arduino to control your Aquaponic or hydroponic farm anyway, since you will probably want to run it for long periods of time, which means that you will want an AC power source instead of batteries anyway.

Purchasing the Arduino

As mentioned previously, there are many manufacturers and retailers of Arduinos. The most reliable source is the Arduino organization itself. This is where you can buy the official versions of the Arduinos, and where you can be sure that you can buy every model. The Web site for this organization is www.arduino.cc. The link near the top labeled Products will drop down a list, which has Arduino at the top. Click on this to go to a chart showing products. You can click on any name, like Uno, to go to the page to describing that product. Click on the SHOP NOW button to go to the purchase page. Note that I am not necessarily recommending that you purchase the products from this organization. You can often get them at a fraction of the price from eBay or Amazon.com. More importantly, as I mentioned previously, sometimes the products you get from third part vendors have significant improvements. The Arduino BUONO available on eBay, for example, accepts a wider range of power supplies. It also provides much more current from the 5V and 3.3V terminals. This is important, because unless you want to provide an additional external power supply for your sensors and other attachments, you will need considerable power for some of these projects. On the other hand, official Arduino products are more likely to be fully compatible with the Arduino IDE (explained next), and might therefore be easier to use for beginners.

Software

In addition to the Arduino hardware, you will need the software used to create software programs (called sketches in the Arduino community) for it. The software you need is the Arduino integrated development environment (IDE). The IDE allows you to write sketches in the programming language called C and then download these sketches onto the Arduino. The IDE must be installed on your computer. In this book, I will be discussing the Windows version, but the differences are minor in the other versions and you should have little problem adapting to the differences.

You can download the IDE from https://www.arduino.cc/en/main/software

Assuming you are running Windows, I recommend that you click on the Windows installer link. This downloads an EXE file that you simply run to install the Arduino IDE on your computer. Once installed, a round icon containing an infinity symbol with + and - signs inside the loops will show on your desktop. Double click this to run the IDE.

When you run the IDE, for the first time, it will bring up an empty sketch with the name "sketch" followed by the current date followed by a letter. The empty sketch appears in the text area of the IDE, and looks like this.

```
void setup() {
  // put your setup code here, to run once:

}

void loop() {
  // put your main code here, to run repeatedly:
```

}

Sketch 1.1

Once you have run the IDE and created and saved sketches, running the IDE will often bring up the most recent sketch it was running. Sometimes it will run several copies of the IDE, each with a different recent sketch in it. You can load the empty sketch at any time by clicking in the File menu on the IDE and then clicking on New, or by simply pressing Ctrl-N when any IDE has the focus in Windows.

This empty sketch contains the basics of an Arduino sketch. Specifically, it contains the two main parts of any Arduino sketch. The setup section (called a "routine") will contain lines of code that initialize or set up the program. After the code in the setup routine is executed, the loop routine is run. The code in the loop section will repeat over and over in a loop for as long as the Arduino is running (powered up). The term void before these two routines simply means that that routine name cannot become any numeric value when it is running. For example, you cannot have code that says X = setup() or X = loop(). This is to distinguish these from other routines that you can write that can take on a value, such as a subroutine (explained shortly) that starts with int instead of void. If that seems confusing, do not worry about it. You will not need a detailed understanding of C programming to use this book.

Before the line that reads "void setup," you will put "include" commands that load files containing code stored in what are called libraries. Some libraries come with the basic IDE and some you will need to download from the Web. You will also put definitions of variables you will use in the sketch. This will be explained in later chapters.

Libraries are collections of code that other people have already written. Most of these are code that allows the Arduino to use devices (such as sensors) that you can attach to the Arduino, and most of it is written by the people who created or sell these devices. You will not need to concern yourself with what is inside these libraries. You only need to know how to obtain them and install them on your computer so they can be loaded by the IDE.

There are two ways to install a library on your computer so that the IDE can access it. The first is to use the Manage Libraries function of the IDE. To do this, click on the Sketch menu item at the top of the IDE screen. Go down the dropdown screen that appears and hover the mouse over "Include Libraries." Another list will appear with "Manage Libraries" at the top. Move the mouse over and click on this. A screen will appear that contains a long list of libraries. You can shorten this list by putting part of the name of the library you are looking for in the box that says "Filter your search," or you can simply scroll down the list until you find the one you are looking for. When you do find the right library, click on the box containing the name and description of the library. A small box labeled "Install" will appear. Click on this to install the library. When I suggest this technique in this book, I will give you as much information as possible on what to look for.

The second way to install a library is to first download the library in the form of a ZIP file onto your computer from a Web site and then install it on the IDE. When you need a library for a project in this book, I will tell you where to find the ZIP file. A ZIP file is a single file containing one or more files in compressed form. Once you have downloaded it onto your computer, you again click on the Sketch menu and hover over "Include Libraries." This time, on the dropdown list that appears, click on "Add ZIP library." A list of folders will appear. Click on the folder that the ZIP file was downloaded into. Usually, this will be the "downloads" folder, but it may vary on your computer. When you click on the folder, you will see a list of ZIP files in that folder. (You may also see a list of subfolders in that folder if you have any there.) Double click on the ZIP file that you just downloaded, or click on the ZIP file and then click on the Open button. This will install the library in the

IDE. Once a library has been installed, you do not need to repeat this process to use it.

Back to Sketch 1.1, you will put code into the void setup routine that sets up the operation. This code will go between the { symbol that appears after "void setup" and the } symbol after this. This type of code would include things like assigning digital connections to be input or output, setting their initial state to be on or off, activating communication channels to be used later, and other basic startup operations. Examples of this will be given when I get into specific sketches later in the book.

It is worth explaining here that whenever you have several lines of code in C that are grouped together, you put the { symbol before these lines of code and the } symbol after them. In fact, even if there is only one line of code but it is in a situation where you could have more than one line, you need to include the {} symbols. For example, you sometimes have a statement called an if statement that causes certain lines to be executed only if a certain condition is true. This would look something like this
if (x > 2) {
    one or more lines of code here
}
This causes the lines of code to be executed only if x is greater than 2. The {} symbols surround all the lines of code that should be executed if that is true. Even if there is only one line of code, you need the {} symbols to should the Arduino that this one line of code is what is executed.

Another example of an important use of the {} symbols is where one or more lines of code will be executed repeatedly in a loop. You surround those lines (or line) with the {} symbols. The main example of a loop is the main loop of the sketch that is automatically executed every time you power up the Arduino. As mentioned previously, the code that goes between void loop() { and the } symbol that goes after it is code that will automatically be repeated the entire time the Arduino is running. This primarily consists of checking inputs and responding to any changes in them.

Note that you can and usually will have {} symbols within other {} symbols. For example, you will often have if statements inside loops. In these cases, the innermost { matches up with the next }, the { before that { matches up with the second }, and so on. It is important to keep track of your {} symbols to make sure they match up. This is one of the hardest and most complicated parts of C programming.

There may be sections of code called subroutines that will be outside of the main loop. These are generally sections of code that might be run repeatedly in different areas of the code. Rather than writing the same code over and over throughout the program, you can put that code in a subroutine and have code that simply jumps to the subroutine, which is called calling the subroutine. After the last line of code in the subroutine, the program returns to where the subroutine was called from, and next line after the subroutine was called is executed. Sometimes, subroutines are included that will only be called from one location, but it is put aside into a subroutine to make it easier to find in you want to make changes in it later. This can be easier than searching through the loop or setup routine that has gotten quite large because of a complex procedure. Subroutines can also be handy in situations like this book, where I might use the same section of code in several chapters, and I want to make it easier for you to copy the same code. Aside from suggesting equipment that you can use with an Arduino in an Aquaponic or hydroponic garden in this book, most of the book will be giving you sketches that you can use, along with information on how to modify the sketches to suit your individual needs.

Connecting your Arduino to your computer

Now that you have the IDE installed, you will need to connect it to your Arduino in order to upload programs to it. There are several steps to this.

First, you need to tell the IDE what type of Arduino you are using. To do this, click on the Tools menu at the top of the IDE screen. Go down and hover over Boards. When a menu with a list of boards appears, move the mouse over and click on the name of your board. The Uno is listed as "Arduino/Genuino Uno." The Mega is listed as "Arduino/Genuino Mega or Mega2560." Once you click on a board, the word "Board" in the list under Tools will have the name of your board beside it.

Next, plug your Arduino into your computer. Use a USB cable, preferably the one that came with your Arduino. Note: If you did not get a cable with your Arduino and you are using another cable, be sure it is a data cable and not just a charging cable. The cables that come with some accessories are for charging the accessories only, and include only the power lines, not the data line. Plug one end into the Arduino and the other into one of the USB ports for your computer. The two ends of the cable are different, and only one end will fit into each of these.

Under the Tools menu on the IDE, you will find "Port." Once you have connected the Arduino to your computer, the IDE will usually automatically connect to the Arduino. The "Port" option on the menu will display what port the Arduino is connected to. For example, it might say "Port: COM4 Arduino/Genuino Uno" instead of just "Port." If this does not happen automatically, go down to the Port option on the menu, then move over to the port that has your board listed next to it. If no port has an Arduino board next to it, you either do not have the Arduino connected properly to your computer (perhaps not a data cable), or it may be a poor quality off brand Arduino, or you have a very old version of the IDE. I recommend at least version 1.8.1 of the IDE. Click on Help and then About to find your version number.

Once you have completed these steps, you are ready to start writing sketches to automate your aquaponic/hydroponic garden and uploading them to your Arduino. You write the sketches in the text area of the IDE then click on the right-pointing arrow near the top of the screen next to the check mark to download the program from the computer onto the Arduino.

Chapter 2

A Simple Timer

One of the simplest things to do with the Arduino is to build a timer. For example, you might want a timer to turn the pumps on and off for your flood and drain aquaponic garden. Of course, you can buy timers for this, but designing your own can give you more flexibility and features. For example, we will discuss later how to have the timer change the timing automatically to water more often in hot, dry weather when the plants might dry out faster. You can also have it operate multiple devices on the same timer, such as have one device go on at the same time as another going off or having different devices go on and off at different times.

In order to control something like a pump with the Arduino, you will need to have the Arduino operate some type of switch, like a relay. Some typical Arduino compatible relays are shown in Figure 2.1.

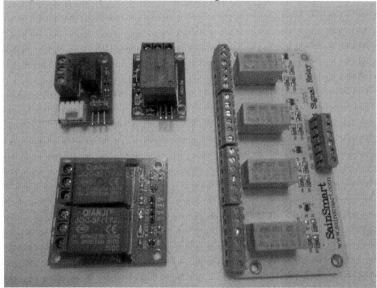

Figure 2.1

This figure shows two relay boards containing a single relay, one board with two relays, and one board with four relays. Relays can be single or double throw and single or double (or more) pole. A double throw relay is one that makes one connection (turns on) when the relay has power and makes another connection when the relay does not have power. That is, it automatically turns one thing on when it turns another thing off. A double pole relay is a relay that turns two different things on (and/or off) at the same time. Double pole relays can also be used to turn on and off one item that draws a lot of current by connecting the same wire to both contacts, distributing the current over both contacts.

Relays specifically designed for Arduinos will generally have separate connections for powering the relay coil and for controlling it. That is, the relay board will have a connection labeled VCC (or just V or + if space is limited on the relay board) and a connection labeled GND (or just G or -). These are for powering the relay coil. You should connect the VCC pin on the relay to your Arduino's 5V connection and the GND pin to one of your Arduino's GND connections. There will also be one or more (depending on how many relays are on the board) relay control connections with labels such as IN1 (for input #1) or S (for signal). You will connect each of these to a different digital output connection on your Arduino, such as D13. The Arduino digital output pin does not therefore actually power the relay, it merely controls it. This is done because the digital outputs of an Arduino may not have enough current to actually power the relay coil directly.

The relay board will also usually have three screw terminals to connect the device you are controlling to. The center one will be the center (common) connection of the relay, one of the side screw connections will be the normally open (unconnected, and therefore off) connection and the other the normally closed (connected when the relay coil is not powered) connection. If the relay is a double pole, it will have six connections. You will probably want to connect wires to the center and normally open terminals, so that no current is flowing when the relay is off. Many devices you will want to control will have a transformer that reduces the outlet power (usually 120 volts or 240 volts) down to a lower voltage like 24 volts or 12 volts. You can use the relay to switch on and off the lower voltage. However, this wastes power because the transformer draws power even if there is no power being drawn from the lower voltage end. It is therefore more energy efficient to cut off the power from the outlet. If you want to do this, one easy way to make a versatile setup is to cut one cord of an extension cord and connect it to the normally open terminals of the relay. This will allow you to plug whatever you want into the extension cord, allowing for easy changing or replacement of components. Figure 2.2 shows this.

Figure 2.2

Note: you should connect the hot wire to the relay, not the neutral wire. If you look closely at a polarized extension cord plug, you will see that it has a narrow prong and a wider prong that will only fit into one of the holes in an outlet. The hot wire is the one that goes to the smaller prong. Of course, it is more complicated if you are using a three wire grounded extension cord, because you must use the correct wire of the three.

You also need to make sure the relay contacts can handle the current your device will draw. Some Arduino controlled relays (including the one shown in Figure 2.2) can handle up to 10 amps at 120 volts, while others can only handle about 1 amp. The ampere rating of a relay is usually stamped on the relay and will be listed in the description of the relay when you buy it. If the equipment you are controlling with the relay gives you its power requirement in watts, you need to convert that to amps to know if your relay can handle it. Power in watts equals the voltage to the device times the current in amps. Thus, if your device runs off 120 volts (normal line output in the US), divide the wattage of the device by 120 to know how many amps it draws. For example, a 200-watt device that runs off 120 volts AC would draw about 1.66 amps, so you should use a relay rated above 1.66 amps. Ratings are usually in even numbers, so you would be looking for a relay rated at a minimum of 2 amps.

You also must provide proper housing for all electrical equipment, especially equipment handling high voltage like this, to protect against rain and other hazards. The examples shown here are for demonstration of basic techniques. It is up to you to ensure that all wiring is properly connected and protected. The author and publisher of this book is not responsible or liable for faulty wiring or workmanship in the construction of any of the projects in this book.

Now that you know how to physically connect the relay to the Arduino, let's look at a simple timer sketch that can turn something on for a set period of time and then off for a set period of time, repeating indefinitely. As mentioned above, an example of such a device would be a pump in a flood and drain system.

```
//Simple timer
// the number of the relay pin
const int relayPin = 13;
// Store start of timing
unsigned long startTime = 0;
unsigned long currentTime;
// initial state of relay is on is false
```

```
bool PowerOn = false;

//How long power is on and off in minutes
long timeOff = 75 * 60 * 1000;
long timeOn = 15 * 60 * 1000;

void setup() {
  // set the digital pin as output and start out as off:
  pinMode(relayPin, OUTPUT);
  digitalWrite(relayPin, LOW );
}

void loop() {
  currentTime = millis();
  if (PowerOn) {
    if (currentTime - startTime > timeOn) {
      digitalWrite(relayPin, LOW );
      startTime = currentTime;
      PowerOn = false;
    }
  } // End of if PowerOn
  if (!PowerOn) {
    if (currentTime - startTime > timeOff) {
      digitalWrite(relayPin, HIGH);
      startTime = currentTime;
      PowerOn = true;
    }
  } // End of if power not on

} // end of loop
```
Sketch 2.1

Let's take a look at this sketch. First, the double slash (//) tells the IDE to ignore the rest of the line when preparing the actual code to send to the Arduino. It is a comment to remind the programmer of something, not actual code.

The line

const int relayPin = 13;
says that relayPin (the number of the output that the relay will be connected to) is a constant (it will not change its value), is an integer, and it is equal to 13. Note that every complete line in this type of code ends with a semicolon, which indicates the end of one command. Failure to include this will result in an error message when you try to send the sketch to the Arduino.

    The line
unsigned long startTime = 0;
says that the variable startTime is an unsigned (will never be negative) long (large) integer, and it starts at value of 0. However, since it is not a constant, it can change within the sketch. The line
unsigned long currentTime;
sets the variable currentTime to be another unsigned long integer, but does to set any specific value to it. This is not a problem, as long as the code does set a value to it somewhere before it tries to read the value of currentTime. The line
bool PowerOn = false;
says that the variable PowerOn (which stores whether the power to the relay is on) is a boolean variable (either true or false, rather than a number value) and starts out false. A variable of this type is sometimes called a flag. The lines
long timeOff = 75 * 60 * 1000;
long timeOn = 15 * 60 * 1000;
set long (large integer) variables timeOff and timeOn. These are the variables that determine how long you want the relay to be off and on, respectively. The unit of measure for the timer is milliseconds (thousandths of a second). Since there are 1000 milliseconds in a second and 60 seconds in a minute, setting timeOff to 75 times 60 times 1000 sets the period of time that the relay is turned off to 75 minutes (1 hour and 15 minutes). Likewise, setting timeOn to 15 times 60 times 1000 milliseconds causes the relay to be turned on for 15 minutes. This part of the sketch is called definitions. Note that this is the part of the code

that you are most likely to want to alter to fit your needs. That is, you can set how long you want the power to be on by changing the 15 to another number of minutes and how long you want the power to be off by changing the 75 to another number of minutes. In this sketch, you would need to actually change the code and reload the program onto the Arduino to change these times. Later, we will discuss ways to change them without reloading the code, or even have them changed automatically to suit current conditions like air temperature and humidity.

The next part of the code is the setup, the part that runs once when the Arduino is first powered up. There are two statements in the setup in this sketch.
pinMode(relayPin, OUTPUT);
digitalWrite(relayPin, LOW);
The first one sets the mode of the relay pin (13) to output mode. As you should recall, each digital pin can be either input or output. The second statement uses the digitalWrite command to send a value of LOW, which mean ground (negative). Sending a value of HIGH would cause this output to go to 5 volts.

Now we come to the most complex part of the code, the part in the loop routine. This is the part that will repeat over and over as long as the Arduino is running. First, the line
currentTime = millis();
sets the value of currentTime to the value of the function millis(). This function is a built-in function that gives the current number of milliseconds the Arduino has been running. It is basically an internal clock in the Arduino. By setting the variable currentTime to this clock, we have a time to use as a reference.

Next, we have a second of code that will only be executed if the variable PowerOn has a value of true. This is controlled by the statement
if (PowerOn) {
The { symbol indicates the start of a section of code. The code between the { and the matching } will only be

executed if the statement within the parentheses following the if is true. The first line in this section tests the time. If the current time minus the start time is greater than the number of minutes you have set for the power to be on (PowerOn), then the code after the line
if (currentTime - startTime >= timeOn) {
and before the matching } symbol will execute. The first line,
digitalWrite(relayPin, LOW);
tells the relay pin to go to the low value (ground), turning off the relay. The next line,
startTime = currentTime;
sets the start time to the current time. This start time will be the time the Arduino starts counting to turn the power back on. The next line,
PowerOn = false;
keeps track of the fact that the power is now off. These are all the lines that are executed when the power is on and the time since the power went on reaches the limit timeOn.

    The next section handles turning the power back on after the set time. This starts with the line
if (!PowerOn) {
This might look like a strange line. However, in the C language an exclamation point means NOT, so the statement means if not PowerOn. Thus, if the power is not currently on, the statements between the { and the matching } will be executed. The first line is familiar.
if (currentTime - startTime > timeOff) {
This again determines if it is time to take action. This time, however, it is checking to see if the time between startTime and currentTime is greater than timeOff, the time the relay should be off. If this is true, the lines
digitalWrite(relayPin, HIGH);
startTime = currentTime;
PowerOn = true;
are executed. The first sets the pin relayPin HIGH, which means 5 volts, turning on the relay. The second resets the start time to the current time, to start the counter for turning

the relay back off again. The third line sets the PowerOn variable to true, to keep track of the fact that the power is currently on.

That is the end of the loop that keeps repeating as long as the Arduino is on. It is really quite simple. Get the current time. If the power is on, check to see if the time since the time it was turned on is more than the time it is supposed to be on. If so, turn the power off, set the start time to the current time so you can keep track of how long the power has been off, and make a note that the power is now off by setting the variable PowerOn to false. If the power is not on, check to see if the power has been off longer than the set time. If so, turn on the power, reset the start time, and note that the power is on by setting PowerOn to true.

There is, unfortunately, one serious flaw in this sketch. The problem is with the built-in function millis(). This function has a maximum value of 4294967296 milliseconds, which is equal to about 49.7 days. After that, it resets to 0 and starts over again. Look at the effect of this. The variable startTime keeps getting increased to the current time when the relay is turned on or off. This only happens when the current time is later than the start time by a set amount. Once millis() drops to 0 and starts recounting and currentTime is set to this, currentTime will always be lower than startTime (which has been set to a very high value when currentTime was close to 4294967296) and the whole operation will stop. The power will stay either on or off, whichever it was when the timer reset to 0. To have the sketch fix this, we need to add a bit of code to check to see if millis() has reset to 0 and fix this. Fortunately, this is a quick fix. The moment millis() resets and currentTime is set to millis(), currentTime will be less than startTime. This can only happen if currentTime jumped backwards. So, we need to add the following lines after the line currentTime = millis();

if (startTime > currentTime) {

```
    startTime = 0;
}
```

What this simply says is that if the start time is larger than the current time, reset the start time to 0 also. This puts the start time back behind the current time. This pretty much fixes the problem, unless your timing is very critical. The only problem is that once every 49.7 days, you will have a slight delay in your operation. Suppose, for example, millis() resets to 0 while the power to the relay has been off for 30 minutes, and you have set the code to turn the power on after 75 minutes. After the reset, the timing will restart from 0, which means that it will be 75 minutes (or whatever value you had timeOff set for) before the power is turned back on. However, since the power had already been off for 30 minutes before the reset, the total time the power was off will be 75 + 30 = 105 minutes. The worst case scenario would be if the reset happened just before the power was due to go on. In that case, the time off for the power would be nearly double the desired time. Likewise, if the power happened to be on when the reset happened, the power would be on for nearly twice the desired time. Of course, this would only happen once every 49.7 days, and it is very unlikely that the reset would happen at the worst possible time (just before a change was supposed to happen). The complete code for this is given in Sketch 2.2.

```
//Simple timer
// the number of the relay pin
const int relayPin = 13;
// Store start of timing
unsigned long startTime = 0;
unsigned long currentTime;
// initial state of relay is on is false
bool PowerOn = false;

//How long power is on and off in minutes
```

```
long timeOff = 75 * 60 * 1000;
long timeOn = 15 * 60 * 1000;

void setup() {
  // set the digital pin as output and start out as off:
  pinMode(relayPin, OUTPUT);
  digitalWrite(relayPin, LOW );
}

void loop() {
  currentTime = millis();
  if (startTime > currentTime) {
    StartTime = 0;
  }
  if (PowerOn) {
    if (currentTime - startTime > timeOn) {
      digitalWrite (relayPin, LOW);
      startTime = currentTime;
      PowerOn = false;
    }
  } // End of if PowerOn
  if (!PowerOn) {
    if (currentTime - startTime > timeOff) {
      digitalWrite(relayPin, HIGH);
      startTime = currentTime;
      PowerOn = true;
    }
  } // End of if power not on
} // end of loop
```
Sketch 2.2

There is an alternative code that solves this problem in a way that the maximum amount of the time glitch (amount of time too long on or off) is about one minute. The code is a bit more complex, and is given in Sketch 2.3.

```
//More complex timer
// the number of the relay pin
const int relayPin = 13;
// initial state of relay is on is false
bool PowerOn = false;
//How long power is on and off in minutes
int TimeOff = 75;
int TimeOn = 15;

unsigned long PreviousTime = 0;
unsigned long TimePassed = 0;

void setup() {
  // set the digital pin as output and start out as off:
  pinMode(relayPin, OUTPUT);
  digitalWrite(relayPin, LOW);
}

void loop() {
  if (millis() < PreviousTime) {PreviousTime = 0;}
  if (millis() - PreviousTime >= 60000) {
    TimePassed = TimePassed + 1;
    PreviousTime = millis();
  }
  if (PowerOn) {
    if (TimePassed >= TimeOn) {
      digitalWrite(relayPin, LOW);
      TimePassed = 0;
      PowerOn = false;
    }
  } // End of if PowerOn
  if (!PowerOn) {
    if (TimePassed >= TimeOff) {
      digitalWrite(relayPin, HIGH);
      TimePassed = 0;
      PowerOn = true;
    }
```

} // End of if power not on
} // end of loop

Sketch 2.3

Here we initialize the program by defining relayPin and PowerOn as before. We define and set TimeOff and TimeOn differently this time. They are expressed as straightforward minutes rather than milliseconds, so the math is simpler and they can be integers because they will not get to be very big. You will, of course, set these for however many minutes you want the power off and on. We define PreviousTime as a long integer. This is equivalent to the variable StartTime from Sketch 2.2. A new variable, TimePassed, is defined as an unsigned long and set to 0. This will keep track of how many minutes have passed. The Setup routine does not change from the previous sketches.

In the loop routine, the line
if (millis() < PreviousTime) {PreviousTime = 0;}
handles the rollover by setting PreviousTime to 0 if it is more than Millis(), indicating that rollover has occurred. The code
 if (millis() - PreviousTime >= 60000) {
  TimePassed = TimePassed + 1;
  PreviousTime = millis();
 }
increases the variable TimePassed by 1 every 60000 milliseconds (60 seconds). The first line simply says that if the current time from the millis() internal clock minus the previous time is equal to or greater than 60000 milliseconds, add one minute to TimePassed and set PreviousTime to the current time. This is like the minute hand on a clock advancing every time the second hand completes a revolution. TimePassed now becomes the timer, expressed in minutes. If PowerOn is true, then if TimePassed is equal to or greater than TimeOff, the relay pin is turned off, TimePassed is set to 0 just as CurrentTime was in previous sketches, and PowerOn is set to false. If the

power was off (!PowerOn) and TimePassed is equal to or more than TimeOff, the power is turned on, TimePassed is set to 0, and PowerOn is set to true. This part of the code is very similar to Sketch 2.2, with currentTime - startTime being replaced by TimePassed.

The code
if (TimePassed >= TimeOn) {
and
if (TimePassed >= TimeOff) {
are triggered if TimePassed is equal to or greater than the limit. Normally, this would be triggered as soon as TimePassed is equal to the limit. The greater than part is just a precaution against something happening that causes TimePassed to get way ahead. I cannot see any circumstance under which that could actually happen in this code, but I am intending for you to be able to modify the code and add to it, so it is best to be safe.

Changes

If you change the 60000 in this code to 1000, the sketch will still work, but time will be in seconds rather than minutes. That is, you can use this same code to time something in seconds rather than minutes will one simple change.

You can have other things happen besides turning the one relay. For example, at the same time as you have the one relay turned off, you can have another one turned on, and vice versa. For example, in a flood and drain system, you might want to open a valve to drain a tank at the same time as you turn off a valve to flood it. This would just be a matter of defining another relay pin (like relayPin2) and adding
digitalWrite(relayPin2, HIGH);
immediately after you have
digitalWrite(relayPin, LOW);
and
digitalWrite(relayPin2, LOW);

immediately after you have
digitalWrite(relayPin, HIGH);
everywhere in your program.

You can have multiple timers within the loop, allowing you to control several totally separate objects with one Arduino. It is just a matter of duplicating most of the code. The code for controlling two relays on separate times is shown in Sketch 2.4.

```
//Double timer
// the number of the relay pins
const int relayPin = 13;
const int relayPin2 = 12;
// initial states of relays are off
bool PowerOn = false;
bool PowerOn2 = false;

//How long power is on and off in minutes
int TimeOff = 75;
int TimeOn = 15;
int TimeOff2 = 720;
int TimeOn2 = 720;

long PreviousTime = 0;
int TimePassed = 0;
int TimePassed2 = 0;

void setup() {
  // set the digital pin as output and start out as off:
  pinMode(relayPin, OUTPUT);
  digitalWrite(relayPin, LOW );
  pinMode(relayPin2, OUTPUT);
  digitalWrite(relayPin2, LOW );
}

void loop() {
  if (millis() < PreviousTime) {PreviousTime = 0;}
  if (millis() - PreviousTime >= 60000) {
```

```
    TimePassed = TimePassed + 1;
    TimePassed2 = TimePassed2 + 1;
    PreviousTime = millis();
  }
  if (PowerOn) {
    if (TimePassed >= TimeOn) {
      digitalWrite(relayPin, LOW );
      TimePassed = 0;
      PowerOn = false;
    }
  } // End of if PowerOn
  if (!PowerOn) {
    if (TimePassed >= TimeOff) {
      digitalWrite(relayPin, HIGH );
      TimePassed = 0;
      PowerOn = true;
    }
  } // End of if power not on

  if (PowerOn2) {
    if (TimePassed2 >= TimeOn2) {
      digitalWrite(relayPin2, LOW );
      TimePassed2 = 0;
      PowerOn2 = false;
    }
  } // End of if PowerOn
  if (!PowerOn2) {
    if (TimePassed2 >= TimeOff2) {
      digitalWrite(relayPin2, HIGH );
      TimePassed2 = 0;
      PowerOn2 = true;
    }
  } // End of if power not on
} // end of loop
```

Sketch 2.4

Here we have defined a second relay pin, a second set of on and off times (set in this case for 720 minutes = 12 hours), a second PowerOn, and a second TimePassed. The only thing we do not need a second of is PreviousTime. Of course, you can do this with as many timers as you want.

In the next chapter, I will discuss how to have your timer adjust automatically to changing conditions, such as decreasing the drained time when the air temperature is high and/or the humidity is low.

Chapter 3

Air Temperature and Humidity

There are various reasons why you might want to monitor the air temperature and humidity in your aquaponic or hydroponic garden. As mentioned previously, you might want to shorten the time between flooding if the air is hot and dry and the roots might dry out faster. If your garden is enclosed, you can turn on a heat if the air gets too cold. If the air gets too hot, you might want to vent the air in an enclosed greenhouse, especially if it is cooler outside, or otherwise cool your garden. In this chapter, I will discuss these.

Obviously, if you are going to monitor air temperature and humidity, you are going to need a specific sensor for this. There are quite a few sensors you can use to monitor temperature. One of the best known is the DHT11, which can measure temperatures from 0 C (32 F) to 50 C (122 F). You can purchase these for a few dollars on eBay or Amazon.com. Two versions of this are shown in figure 3.1.

Figure 3.1

The one on the left is the basic component, the one on the right is the basic unit packaged with a few additional components. You will at first notice that the one on the right has four pins, while the one on the left has three. However, if you look closely, you will see that the one on the left actually has four connections going into the backing. The third pin from the left (as shown in this picture) of the four pins is not used. On the basic component, the first pin on the left goes to 5V, the second pin is the output which goes to a digital input on the Arduino, and the pin on the right goes to GND. When using this basic unit, you should also connect a resistor between the output and 5V. This resistor is called a pull-up resistor because it pulls the input pin to the 5 volt high value unless the sensor makes a stronger connection to ground. The value of this resistor should be between 4.7 K and 10K. On the three-pin package, this is built in so you do not need to provide it. On this package, which pin goes to which Arduino connection varies with the manufacturer. On the one in the picture, the output is the pin on the left, 5V is the middle pin, and the right pin goes to GND. However, I also have a package where the left pin is GND, the middle pin is output, and the right pin goes to 5V, so check your package carefully. Usually at least two are labeled. Output is often labeled S and GND as -.

Let's suppose, as an example, you want to turn on a heater if the air temperature in your enclosed aquaponic garden gets too low and turn on a cooler if it gets too high. Sketch 3.1 shows some code to do this with this sensor.

```
#include <dht.h>
dht DHT;

#define inputPin 5
#define HeaterPin 6
#define CoolerPin 7

float tempC;
float tempF;
const float upperLimit = 100;
const float lowerLimit = 34;

void setup(){
  pinMode(HeaterPin, OUTPUT);
  digitalWrite(HeaterPin, LOW);
  pinMode(CoolerPin, OUTPUT);
  digitalWrite(CoolerPin, LOW);
}

void loop(){
  int error = DHT.read11(inputPin);
  if (error == 0){
  tempC = DHT.temperature;
  tempF = (tempC * 1.8) + 32.0;
  if (tempF < lowerLimit) {
     digitalWrite(HeaterPin, HIGH);
     }
  else {
```

```
      digitalWrite(HeaterPin, LOW);
    }

  if (tempF > upperLimit){
    digitalWrite(CoolerPin, HIGH);
    }
  else {
    digitalWrite(CoolerPin, LOW);
    }
  } // End of if error == 0
 delay(2000);
} // End of loop
```
                    Sketch 3.1

    The first thing you need to do is download the DHT11 library. You can download the one used for the above sketch here.
https://arduino-info.wikispaces.com/DHT11-Humidity-TempSensor
or
https://arduino-info.wikispaces.com/file/detail/DHT-lib.zip
or
https://app.box.com/s/sj4d9oafq0p7b41zgxtn1w4dswhiagzi

    Install the library as described in Chapter 1. You can also use the library manager as described in Chapter 1. You can type DHT in the filter box to speed your search for the correct library to install, since that will display very few libraries. Note that there are actually several libraries for the temperature sensor. The one you want for the sketch above is the one titled DHTlib.
    The line
#include <dht.h>
loads the library into your sketch and the line
dht DHT;
activates the library for the Arduino.
    The line
#define inputPin 5

sets the sensor input pin to 5, although it can be any digital pin you want to use. The lines

#define HeaterPin 6
#define CoolerPin 7

set the pins that will control the relay for the heater and fan, respectively. (Again, you can pick any pins you want to use.)

We have a few variables and constants to define. The float (floating point, which means they can take on decimal values like 42.5) variables tempC and tempF will be the temperature in Centigrade (AKA Celsius) and Fahrenheit. I will have the program compute both of these just to make it easy for you to use whichever you prefer. The float constants upperLimit and lowerLimit will be set to the temperatures you want to trigger an action. In this example, I have set these for 100 and 34. In this sketch, I will use the tempF variable for comparisons, so these temperatures are in Fahrenheit. One minor point to note: The DHT11 gives temperature and humidity in integer values, so using float variables may seem unnecessary. However, it does make the temperatures more accurate when you convert Celsius to Fahrenheit.

The setup routine sets the digital pins you will attach the relays to the output pins, and sets them to LOW (off) initially. In the main loop, the sketch uses the function DHT.read11(inputPin) to read the sensor. This function returns an error code as an integer, which in this sketch is stored in the variable named error. If the value is 0, there was no error and the temperature and humidity have been read correctly. Values such as -1 and -2 are returned for errors such as checksum error and timeout. Notice that the if (error == 0) test uses two = signs, which in C programming language means "test for equality," as opposed to "make equal." The program will only analyze the data if there was no error. If the data had an error, the loop simply repeats until good data is obtained.

When the sensor is read by the DHT.read11 function, the data is stored in variables like

DHT.temperature. The statement tempC = DHT.temperature loads the temperature into the variable tempC (sets tempC equal to DHT.temperature). Note that the readings from the DHT are in Celsius. The next line computes the Fahrenheit from this and stores it in tempF. You do not have to do this if you are comfortable working in Celsius and used Celsius values for upperLimit and lowerLimit, but I am providing this for people who prefer to work in Fahrenheit.

Now that we have the temperature, we test to see if it is too high or low. The line
if (tempF < lowerLimit) {
tests to see if it is below the temperature you specified as minimum temperature. If it is, the line
digitalWrite(HeaterPin, HIGH);
turns on the heater. The next line is the closing } to indicate the end of the if condition. This is followed by the lines
 else {
   digitalWrite(HeaterPin, LOW);
   }
When you follow an if statement by an else statement, the else statement is executed if the if statement is not true. Thus, in this case, if the temperature is not below the allowable threshold, the else statement turns off the heater. This is important. Remember that the if statement turned on the heater when the temperature got too hot by setting the pin HeaterPin to HIGH (on). However, it would stay HIGH even when the if statement is no longer being activated. That is, a pin set HIGH does not automatically go LOW (off) on its own. This else statement turns the heater back off once the temperature cools off. In the same way, the statements
   if (tempF > upperLimit){
     digitalWrite(CoolerPin, HIGH);
     }
   else {
     digitalWrite(CoolerPin, LOW);
     }

turn the fan or other cooling system on if the temperature gets too high and turn it off again once the cooler has cooled it down. The cooler can be some type of mister to spray water into the air, or an exhaust fan if you have an enclosed greenhouse, or whatever is appropriate for your system.

The statement delay(2000); causes the program flow to stop for 2000 milliseconds (2 seconds). This is done because the sensor needs a few seconds to take a reading. If you try to execute the DHT.read11 function too frequently, you will get erratic results.

At this point, I would like to mention a useful diagnostic tool for those readers not familiar with Arduino code. That is the Serial.print statement. If you look under the tools menu of the Arduino IDE, you will see the item Serial Monitor. If you click on this after you have connected your Arduino to the computer and confirmed that the IDE has located and connected to the COM port for the Arduino, it will display a screen with a large text box. When the Arduino is running code and it hits a Serial.print statement, it will send whatever it is told to print to your computer by the USB cable, and it will show in this screen. To use this, you must put the command
Serial.begin(9600);
In the Setup routine. Then you put commands line
Serial.print("Temperature =");
Serial.println(tempF);
in the code anywhere you want information displayed in the serial monitor box. The first line prints the text "Temperature =". The second line prints the value of the variable tempF. Notice that the command in the second line is println, not print. The difference is that Serial.print leaves the print cursor at the end of whatever was printed, so the next thing printed will be immediately after that. The command Serial.println tells the serial monitor to go to the next line. In short, the println adds a line carriage return and line feed. In this sketch, you could add these two lines immediately after the line

tempF = (tempC * 1.8) + 32.0;
to display the reading in the serial monitor. This will show you if everything is working properly when you load the sketch into your Arduino. If you get crazy numbers for the temperature, you will know that you have a loose connection to your sensor or other problem. When you disconnect the Arduino from the computer, the Serial.print commands simply stop working. However, you might want to remove or remark out these diagnostic lines when you are finished testing and ready to put your circuit into the field. In some of the following examples, I will include these lines where appropriate to help you confirm that your circuit and code are working properly.

    There is one small flaw in the code in Sketch 3.1. The heater or cooler is turned off as soon as the temperature crosses the threshold. This could cause the heater or cooler to frequently switch on and off as soon as the temperature drifts back up or down. To solve this, it can be a good idea to provide some lag time by providing a margin between the on and off temperatures. Sketch 3.2 does this.

```
#include <dht.h>
dht DHT;

#define inputPin 5
#define HeaterPin 6
#define CoolerPin 7

float tempC;
float tempF;
const float upperLimit = 100;
const float lowerLimit = 34;

void setup(){
  pinMode(HeaterPin, OUTPUT);
  digitalWrite(HeaterPin, LOW);
  pinMode(CoolerPin, OUTPUT);
```

```
    digitalWrite(CoolerPin, LOW);
    Serial.begin(9600);
}

void loop(){
  int error = DHT.read11(inputPin);
  if (error == 0){
    tempC = DHT.temperature;
    tempF = (tempC * 1.8) + 32.0;
    Serial.print("Temperature =");
    Serial.println(tempF);

    if (tempF < lowerLimit) {
       digitalWrite(HeaterPin, HIGH);
       }
    if (tempF > lowerLimit + 3) {
       digitalWrite (HeaterPin, LOW);
       }

    if (tempF > upperLimit){
       digitalWrite(CoolerPin, HIGH);
       }
    if (tempF < upperLimit - 3){
       digitalWrite(CoolerPin, LOW);
       }
  } // End of if error == 0
  delay(2000);
} // End of loop
```
Sketch 3.2

This is the same as Sketch 3.1, except the else statements have been replaced by additional if statements. The
```
else {
    digitalWrite(HeaterPin, LOW);
    }
```
lines have been replaced with
`if (tempF > lowerLimit + 3) {`

```
   digitalWrite(HeaterPin, LOW);
}
```
This turns the heater off when the temperature gets to 3 degrees above the temperature that turned on the heater, rather than immediately as soon as it gets above the lower limit. This means that the heater will continue to heat the air for a while after the temperature has reached the point that turned on the heater. This prevents the heater from turning on and then off every few seconds as the temperature is raised above the lowerLimit temperature and then drops back to below this temperature as soon as the heater goes off. Likewise, the lines
```
else {
   digitalWrite(CoolerPin, LOW);
}
```
have been replaced by
```
if (tempF < upperLimit - 3) {
  digitalWrite(CoolerPin, LOW);
}
```
so that the cooler does not stop until the temperature is 3 degrees below the temperature that triggered it. The number 3 is an arbitrary number. You can use any number you want instead of 3, depending on how close you want the temperature to stay to the trigger points. There is really nothing wrong with Sketch 3.1, as long as you do not mind the heater of cooler switching on and off a lot. Actually, there are some circumstances where you might want the action to stop immediately. For example, instead of turning on a heater when the temperature drops to just above freezing, you might want to turn on the pumps in a flood and drain system. Keeping a flow of water going to the plant roots in this way can keep the roots from freezing, as long as the freezing temperature does not keep up long enough to freeze the entire tank. You can choose whether to use Sketch 3.1 or 3.2, depending on your circumstances.

The DHT sensor shown does not just measure temperature. It also measures humidity. Just as you used the DHT.temperature variable that was loaded when you used the DHT.read11 function, you can also read DHT.humidity to see if the air is getting too dry. I mentioned previously that you might want to adjust the frequency of the flooding in a flood and drain system if the air got too hot and dry, because it the air is both hot and dry the roots of your plants might dry out and be damaged while the water is drained. Sketch 3.3 shows how to do that.

// Self adjusting timer

```
#include <dht.h>
dht DHT;

// the number of the relay pin
const int relayPin = 13;
const int inputPin = 5;
const float TemperatureUpperLimit1= 80;
const float HumidityLowerLimit1 = 40;
const float TemperatureUpperLimit2 = 90;
const float HumidityLowerLimit2 = 35;

// initial state of relay is on is false
bool PowerOn = false;
float tempC;
float tempF;
float HumidityReading;

//How long power is on and off in minutes
int TimeOff = 75;
int TimeOn = 15;

long PreviousTime = 0;
int TimePassed = 0;

void setup() {
  // set the digital pin as output and start out as off:
  pinMode(relayPin, OUTPUT);
```

```
  digitalWrite(relayPin, LOW);
  Serial.begin(9600);
}

void loop() {
  int TimeOff = 75;
  int error = DHT.read11(inputPin);
  if (error == 0){
   tempC = DHT.temperature;
   tempF = (tempC * 1.8) + 32.0;
   HumidityReading = DHT.humidity;
    if   (tempF   >   TemperatureUpperLimit1   &&
HumidityReading < HumidityLowerLimit1) {
     TimeOff = 60;
    }
    if   (tempF   >   TemperatureUpperLimit2   &&
HumidityReading < HumidityLowerLimit2) {
     TimeOff = 45;
    }
  }
  Serial.print("Temp = ");
  Serial.print(tempF);
  Serial.print("  Hum = ");
  Serial.print(HumidityReading);
  Serial.print("  Time = ");
  Serial.println(TimeOff);

  if (millis() < PreviousTime) {PreviousTime = 0;}
  if (millis() - PreviousTime >= 60000) {
   TimePassed = TimePassed + 1;
   PreviousTime = millis();
  }

  if (PowerOn) {
   if (TimePassed >= TimeOn) {
    digitalWrite(relayPin, LOW);
    TimePassed = 0;
    PowerOn = false;
```

```
    }
  } // End of if PowerOn
  if (!PowerOn) {
    if (TimePassed >= TimeOff) {
      digitalWrite(relayPin, HIGH);
      TimePassed = 0;
      PowerOn = true;
    }
  } // End of if power not on
  delay(2000);
} // end of loop
```
Sketch 3.3

This combines Sketch 2.3 and Sketch 3.2. We load and activate the DHT library with
#include <dht.h>
and
dht DHT;
respectively. We select the relay pin that will control the pump and the input pin for the temperature and humidity sensor with the lines
const int relayPin = 13;
const int inputPin = 5;

We then set the trigger points for temperature and humidity with the lines
const float TemperatureUpperLimit1= 80;
const float HumidityLowerLimit1 = 40;
const float TemperatureUpperLimit2 = 90;
const float HumidityLowerLimit2 = 35;

Unlike the previous sketches involving the temperature sensor, we are setting limits for humidity in addition to temperature. We are also setting two limits for each. This will allow you to adjust the off periods of the pump for three different conditions: under 80 degrees F, between 80 and 90 degrees F, and over 90 degrees F. You can actually set as many of these trip points as you like. I have simply chosen two for demonstration purposes. You can also select whatever temperatures and humidities you feel appropriate for your system. The values selected here are arbitrary.

Next, we define the same variables used in sketches 2.3 and 3.2, and added HumidityReading to store the humidity reading. The setup routine is the same as Sketch 2.3, setting up the relay pin to control the pump.

The main difference comes in the loop routine. Sketch 3.3 is most like the timer sketch 2.3, so I will discuss the differences between Sketches 2.3 and 3.3. In the loop routine, we first set the TimeOff variable to 75, the value we set it for if the temperature is normal. Then we use the line
int error = DHT.read11(inputPin);
to read the temperature and humidity. If there is no error, we store these in tempC, tempF, and HumidityReading. Then we use the line

if (tempF > TemperatureUpperLimit1 &&
HumidityReading < HumidityLowerLimit1) {

to compare the temperature and humidity to the first set of limits. In the C programming language, the symbol && mean AND, so this line in plain English reads "If temperature in Fahrenheit is greater than temperature upper limit 1 and humidity reading is lower than humidity lower limit 1 then do what it says until the next } symbol." What it says before the next } symbol is
TimeOff = 60;
which sets the timeOff period to 60 minutes instead of the 75 minutes it had previously been set to. After this, we have another if statement that says

if (tempF > TemperatureUpperLimit2 &&
HumidityReading < HumidityLowerLimit2) {

This is the same thing, except it checks to see if the temperature is higher than upper limit 2 instead of 1 and the

humidity is lower than lower limit 2. If these conditions are met, it executes the command
TimeOff = 45;
which lowers the time off period further to 45 minutes.

After this, the loop routine is the same as the simple timer, except for the delay command at the end of the loop to slow down the reading of the sensor. The code calculates TimePassed the same way as before, and if the power is off and TimePassed is greater than the TimeOff value, it turns on the pump.

Let's be clear on what is happening here. Each time the loop starts, it first sets the TimeOff to the maximum value, 75 minutes (or whatever you want the normal delay time to be). Then it checks to see if the mildest combination of adverse temperature and humidity conditions is true. If so, it reduces the TimeOff to 60 minutes. (Again, you can make this whatever you think is suitable for your system.) Then it checks to see if temperature and humidity conditions are even worse, and if so, sets the TimeOff even lower. You can have as many of these steps as you want. It is very important, however, to remember to start with the mildest conditions and proceed to the more severe ones. If you had them out of order, it would set the TimeOff to a very short time when it found very severe conditions, but then when you tested for less severe conditions it would find that these were satisfied too and reset the TimeOff to a longer time again. So, test for progressively worse conditions.

It might seem odd to keep changing the TimeOff value. Remember, however, that the value of TimeOff has no actual effect until the program gets to the point in the code where it compares TimeOff to TimePassed. The code can change it all it wants until it gets to that point with no effect.

In this example, I have used a combination of temperature and humidity to trigger a change in the TimeOff for the pump. You can change these conditions as you see fit for your system. You may decide to use only temperature, or only humidity, or some different combination of these. This example is intended as much to demonstrate a principle that you can build on as to provide specific code.

The previous examples used the DHT11 sensor. A similar temperature sensor you can use is the DHT22. This is slightly more expensive, but is more accurate, giving the temperature and humidity to one decimal place rather than as integers. In addition, it has a temperature range from -40 C (-40 F) to 80 C (174 F), which can be more useful than the DHT11 for measuring temperature extremes. The DHT22 looks similar to the DHT11, except that the DHT11 is usually blue while the DHT22 is usually white, and the pin connections (5V, output, and GND) are the same. From a hardware standpoint, you can swap a DHT22 with a DHT11 with no changes. However, the drivers are a little different and thus the code is too. Sketch 3.4 shows the code from Sketch 3.3 modified to use the DHT22.

You can download the library used in this sketch (Arduino-DHT22-master.zip) from
https://github.com/ringerc/Arduino-DHT22
or
https://app.box.com/s/pjt1f2vtdvgwmvvrs88hrihj8oi88vmc
You can also use the Manage Library function as explained in Chapter 1 to load the library. Type DHT22 in the filter box to limit the libraries displayed and select the Arduino-DHT22-Master library to load.

```
#include <DHT22.h>

#define DHT22_PIN 5
DHT22 myDHT22(DHT22_PIN);

const int relayPin = 13;
const float TemperatureUpperLimit1 = 80;
const float HumidityLowerLimit = 40;
const float TemperatureUpperLimit2 = 90;
const float HumidityLowerLimit2 = 35;
```

```cpp
// initial state of relay is on is false
bool PowerOn = false;
float tempC;
float tempF;
float HumidityReading;

//How long power is on and off in minutes
int TimeOff = 75;
int TimeOn = 15;

long PreviousTime = 0;
int TimePassed = 0;

void setup() {
  // set the digital pin as output and start out as off:
  pinMode(relayPin, OUTPUT);
  digitalWrite(relayPin, LOW );
  Serial.begin(9600);
}

void loop() {
  TimeOff = 75;
  DHT22_ERROR_t error;
  error = myDHT22.readData();
  if (error == 0){
   tempC = myDHT22.getTemperatureC();
   tempF = (tempC * 1.8) + 32.0;
   HumidityReading = myDHT22.getHumidity();
if (tempF > TemperatureUpperLimit1 &&
HumidityReading < HumidityLowerLimit) {
    TimeOff = 60;
     } // End first test
   if (tempF > TemperatureUpperLimit2 &&
HumidityReading < HumidityLowerLimit2) {
    TimeOff = 45;
     } //End second test
  } // End if error == 0
```

```
Serial.print("Temp = ");
Serial.print(tempF);
Serial.print("  Hum = ");
Serial.print(HumidityReading);
Serial.print("  Time = ");
Serial.println(TimeOff);
if (millis() < PreviousTime) {PreviousTime = 0;}
if (millis() - PreviousTime >= 60000) {
  TimePassed = TimePassed + 1;
  PreviousTime = millis();
}

if (PowerOn) {
  if (TimePassed >= TimeOn) {
    digitalWrite(relayPin, LOW );
    TimePassed = 0;
    PowerOn = false;
  }
} // End of if PowerOn
if (!PowerOn) {
  if (TimePassed >= TimeOff) {
    digitalWrite(relayPin, HIGH );
    TimePassed = 0;
    PowerOn = true;
  }
} // End of if power not on
delay(3000);
}
```

Sketch 3.4

The functioning of this code is exactly the same as Sketch 3.3 for the DHT11. The only changes are the exact wording of the statements to accommodate the different library. For example, DHT.temperature is replaced with myDHT22.getTemperatureC()
and int error = DHT.read11(inputPin) is replaced by the two lines DHT22_ERROR_t error and error =

myDHT22.readData(). Of course, the include statement #include <dht.h> has been changed to #include <DHT22.h> and dht DHT has been changed to
DHT22 myDHT22(DHT22_PIN). You might notice that the delay has been increased from 2000 milliseconds to 3000 milliseconds. This sensor takes a little longer to read, probably because of the greater accuracy.

Chapter 4

Water Temperature

More important than air temperature in most aquaponic systems is the water temperature. This is very similar to getting the air temperature. However, we will use a different temperature sensor and set of libraries. While we used the DHT11 or DHT22 sensors, which can measure both temperature and humidity, for air, we will use the DS18B20 sensor for water. This sensor is readily available as a waterproof probe with 1 to 3 meter length cables. You can, of course, always add longer wires to the cables if you need to. Of course, it is best to get a longer cable if you want to place the sensor deep underwater so there is no chance of water getting into your homemade connections. Figure 4.1 shows the typical sensor.

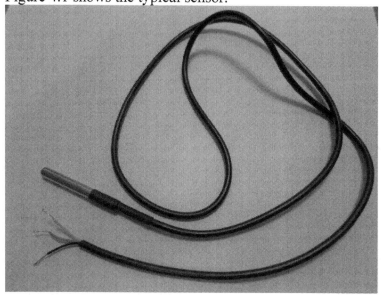

Figure 4.1

It has three wires. The red wire should be connected to your Arduino 5 V connection and the black wire to one of the GND connections. The yellow wire goes to whichever digital input pin you want to use. You do need to connect a resistor with a value from about 4.7 K to 10 K between the red and yellow wires in addition to connecting these wires to 5 V and the input connection. To put it another way, you need to connect the Arduino analog input pin you select for this sensor to the 5 V connection with a 4.7 to 10 K resistor. This is called a pull-up resistor. If you do not include this resistor, or if any of the connections are loose, the sensor will always read negative 175 C, regardless of the temperature.

In order to use this type of sensor, you will need to add two libraries to the Arduino IDE if it does not already have them. The first is the OneWire library, and the other is the DallasTemperature library. The OneWire library, which allows you to connect multiple sensors to one Arduino input pin, can be downloaded from https://github.com/PaulStoffregen/OneWire
or
https://github.com/ntruchsess/arduino-OneWire
The DallasTemperature library can be downloaded from https://github.com/milesburton/Arduino-Temperature-Control-Library
Once you download them, you can install them as explained in Chapter 1.

You can also install them using the Manage Libraries function as explained in Chapter 1. For the OneWire library, I recommend that you put OneWire in the filter box and install the library simply labeled OneWire. For the DallasTemperature library, I recommend that you put DallasTemperature in the filter box and select the library labeled DallasTemperature.

Sketch 4.1 shows how to use this sensor to turn on heating when the water gets too cold and cooling when it gets too hot. It is similar to Sketch 3.2.

```
#include <OneWire.h>
#include <DallasTemperature.h>
```

```
#define ONE_WIRE_BUS 2
#define HeaterPin 13
#define CoolerPin 12
const float upperLimit = 85;
const float lowerLimit = 40;
float tempC;
float tempF;

OneWire oneWire(ONE_WIRE_BUS);
DallasTemperature sensors(&oneWire);

void setup(void) {
  pinMode(HeaterPin, OUTPUT);
  digitalWrite(HeaterPin, LOW );
  pinMode(CoolerPin, OUTPUT);
  digitalWrite(CoolerPin, LOW );
  sensors.begin();
  Serial.begin(9600);
} // End of setup

void loop(void) {
  sensors.requestTemperatures();
  tempC = sensors.getTempCByIndex(0);
  tempF = (tempC * 1.8) + 32.0;
  Serial.print("Temperature =");
  Serial.println(tempF);
  if (tempF < lowerLimit) {
     digitalWrite(HeaterPin, HIGH );
     }
  if (tempF > lowerLimit + 3) {
     digitalWrite(HeaterPin, LOW );
     }

  if (tempF > upperLimit){
     digitalWrite(CoolerPin, HIGH );
     }
  if (tempF < upperLimit - 3){
     digitalWrite(CoolerPin, LOW );
```

}
  delay(1000);
} // End of loop

Sketch 4.1

First, we load the OneWire and DallasTemperature libraries. Then the statement
#define ONE_WIRE_BUS 2
defines ONE_WIRE_BUS to mean 2. This will be the input for the yellow wire of the sensor. You can, of course, select any of the digital pins as your input. We then define HeaterPin, CoolerPin, upperLimit, lowerLimit, tempC, and tempF as we did in previous sketches. Next, the statement
OneWire oneWire(ONE_WIRE_BUS);
sets the input to the pin which ONE_WIRE_BUS was set to, which was 2. We could have just omitted the statement that defined ONE_WIRE_BUS as 2 and used the statement
OneWire oneWire(2);
However, giving numbers names like this at the beginning of a sketch is good programming practice because it allows you to easily find these values all in one place at the beginning of the sketch instead of needing to search the entire sketch to remind yourself, for example, what pin you are using for input. The statement
DallasTemperature sensors(&oneWire);
defines sensors for the DallasTemperature function.

In the setup routine, the pins for the heater and cooler are set to output mode and initially set to LOW (off). The statement
sensors.begin();
activates the reading of the sensors. It does not actually read any sensors, it merely opens the channel to them.

Now we come to the loop routine, where the activity really happens. The command
sensors.requestTemperatures();
loads the temperature readings into variables, just as DHT.read11 did with the DHT sensors. The statement

tempC = sensors.getTempCByIndex(0);
loads the value of variable sensors.getTempCByIndex(0) into variable tempC. Notice the 0. This is because, as mentioned previously, the OneWire library allows you to connect more than one sensor to the same input pin. If you have more than one, the second one would be sensors.getTempCByIndex(1), the third one would be sensors.getTempCByIndex(2), and so on.

From here on, the sketch is almost exactly like Sketch 3.2, even though you are measuring water temperature instead of air temperature. The statement
tempF = (tempC * 1.8) + 32.0;
converts the temperature from Celsius to Fahrenheit and stores the value in tempF. The sketch then compares the temperature to the lower and upper limits a turns on the heater or cooler, respectively. What this does depends on your system. The cooler can be a fan blowing across the top of your fish tank, for example, or something more elaborate.

The serial print statements are there to allow you to confirm that everything is working properly. As mentioned previously, if you have any loose connections, you will probably get readings of -175 C or some other ridiculously low number.

Chapter 5

Water Level

Since aquaponics involves large tanks of water, you often need to monitor the water levels. Usually, the problem is that water levels can get too low due to evaporation, leakage, or simply water being consumed by the products you are growing. There can also be problems with water levels getting too high. This can happen if your system is exposed to rain, but also due to a malfunction of the pumping system.

There are many ways to monitor water levels. Probably the most commonly used way is with float switches. Another way is by having wires in the water that make electrical contact when the water level reaches the level of the wires. Another method that is not as commonly known but is growing in popularity is to have a sonic range finder pointed at the water and have it monitor the distance from the range finder to the top of the water. This method has several advantages. One is that it actually gives you a precise report on the water level, rather than a yes/no response to whether the water level is too high or low. This can be useful if you want the Arduino to actually report the water level to you, instead of just taking action automatically. This will be discussed in later chapters. Another advantage to the ultrasonic range finder is that it is not submerged in the water, so there is no danger shorting out the circuit or problems with corrosion, algae, or other problems associated with keeping an object in the water

An ultrasonic range finder sensor is shown in Figure 5.1.

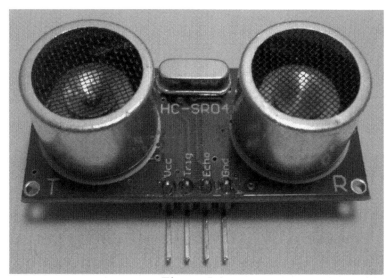

Figure 5.1

This device (which costs a few dollars on eBay or Amazon.com) sends a sound pulse out the speaker, which bounces back and is picked up by the microphone. By measuring the time it takes for the sound to come back, it can measure the distance to the nearest object in front of it. It has a maximum range of about 13 feet, but works best at ranges of a few inches or feet. Placing this sensor pointing down a few inches above the highest water level gives good readings of the distance to the water. Figure 5.2 shows a possible structure for holding the sensor.

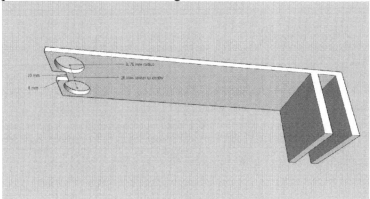

Figure 5.2

The holes are about 8.75 mm in radius and 26 mm from center to center. The notch on the left is 8 mm deep and 10 mm wide, and is for the protruding component between the microphone and speaker. The brace on the right of the picture would go on the side of a tank, and the spacing between them would depend on the thickness of your tank walls. The sensor is then placed on top with the speaker and microphone going through the holes, pointing down. Of course, this is just a suggestion. You can use any method of mounting the sensor that fits your tank.

Figure 5.3 shows the sensor mounted on this holder. This holder was 3D printed, but there are many ways to make this.

Figure 5.3

Let's assume that you want to drain the tank if it gets too high and add water if it gets too low. You can do this with a pump or a valve that you can open electrically. Sketch 5.1 shows how to do this. From the standpoint of the sketch, it does not matter what mechanism you are using to adjust the water level, as long as it is activated by turning on a relay.

```
#define DrainPin 13
#define AddWaterPin 12
#define echoSensorPin 7
#define triggerPin 8
const float LowWaterDistance = 14;
const float HighWaterDistance = 6;

float Duration, Distance;
```

```
void setup(){
  Serial.begin(9600);
  pinMode(echoSensorPin, INPUT);
  pinMode(triggerPin, OUTPUT);
  pinMode(DrainPin, OUTPUT);
  digitalWrite(DrainPin, LOW);
  pinMode(AddWaterPin, OUTPUT);
  digitalWrite(AddWaterPin, LOW);
}// End setup

void loop() {
  digitalWrite(triggerPin, LOW);
  delayMicroseconds(5);
  digitalWrite(triggerPin, HIGH);
  delayMicroseconds(10);
  digitalWrite(triggerPin, LOW);
  Duration = pulseIn(echoSensorPin, HIGH);
  Distance = (Duration /2)/74;
  Serial.print("Distance = ");
  Serial.println(Distance);
   if (Distance < HighWaterDistance) {
     digitalWrite(DrainPin, HIGH);
     }
   if (Distance > HighWaterDistance + 1) {
     digitalWrite(DrainPin, LOW);
     }

   if (Distance > LowWaterDistance){
     digitalWrite(AddWaterPin, HIGH);
     }
   if (Distance < LowWaterDistance - 1){
     digitalWrite(AddWaterPin, LOW);
     }
  delay(500);
} // End main loop
```

Sketch 5.1

First we define the Arduino pins that will be for the pump or valves to lower and raise the water level and the pins used by the sensor, triggerPin and echoSensorPin. Next we set the distance from the sensor for acceptable low and high water levels, the trip points where action will be taken. These statements are

const float LowWaterDistance = 14;
const float HighWaterDistance = 6;

These can be in inches or centimeters. We then define (but do not assign values to) two variables used in finding the distance to the water, Duration and Distance. Duration is the time between a sound pulse being sent out by the sensor and the time it returns. Distance is the distance measured. In this sketch, that distance is measured in inches. If you prefer to work in centimeters, multiply that number by 2.54. The Setup loop then starts the serial communications for debugging purposes, sets the echoSensorPin for input, and sets DrainPin, AddWaterPin, and triggerPin as output pins. It also sets DrainPin and AddWaterPin to low (off). It is not necessary to do this with triggerPin, because this will be set low in the loop routine immediately.

In the loop routine, we set triggerPin low, delay 5 microseconds, set triggerPin high, delay 10 microseconds, and then set triggerPin low again. This sends out the sound pulse. Then the statement

Duration = pulseIn(echoSensorPin, HIGH);

gets the amount of time it took for the pulse to be bounced back. Then the statement

Distance = (Duration /2)/74;

Performs a simple calculation to convert this timer interval to distance in inches. As stated before, you can multiple this by 2.54 if you prefer to work on centimeters. We then send this measurement to the serial port to be displayed on your computer so you can confirm that you are getting accurate measurements for diagnostic purposes. You can delete or remark out the Serial print lines later if you wish.

Next we have the familiar if statements that turn on the relays to power adding or draining water. First you have the statement to turn on the drain if the water distance to the top of the water is less than HighWaterDistance, the minimum acceptable distance to the top of the water. This is followed by the if statement to turn the drain off again when the water level has dropped by one inch. Of course, you replace the one inch with any number of inches you want, even fractions of inches like 1.5. This is followed by an if statement that turns on water to add water if the water is too low (the distance to the top of the water is too high), and the if statement to turn off the water flow when the water has come up another inch. After this we have a delay of 500 milliseconds before testing it again. This is an arbitrary delay, and I inserted it mostly so that the numbers did not scroll by too fast when looking at them on the serial monitor. It does, however, also give any sound bouncing around time to dissipate so you do not get false readings, so it is worth including.

There is a small problem with this code. The ultrasonic range finder occasionally gives a false reading due to vibrations, wind, electrical surges, or other random events. The water could also be disturbed by wind or fish movements. These instances could cause the DrainPin or AddWaterPin to activate. Of course, they will deactivate on the next time around the loop if the water level is more than one inch beyond the activating condition, but it would be better if you did not have even a momentary flicker of power. The solution to this is to require several high or low water readings in a row before a pin is set high, turning on a relay. You would also want to have several not too high or not too low readings in a row before turning off the drain or water addition. This makes the code quite a bit more complicated, but you may consider it worth it. Sketch 5.2 shows how to do this.

```
#define DrainPin 13
#define AddWaterPin 12
#define echoSensorPin 7
#define triggerPin 8
```

```
const float LowWaterDistance = 14;
const float HighWaterDistance = 6;
float Duration, Distance;

unsigned long TooHighCount = 0;
unsigned long NotTooHighCount = 0;
unsigned long TooLowCount = 0;
unsigned long NotTooLowCount = 0;
bool Draining = false;
bool Adding = false;
int MinCount = 4;

void setup() {
  Serial.begin(9600);
  pinMode(echoSensorPin, INPUT);
  pinMode(triggerPin, OUTPUT);
  pinMode(DrainPin, OUTPUT);
  digitalWrite(DrainPin, LOW);
  pinMode(AddWaterPin, OUTPUT);
  digitalWrite(AddWaterPin, LOW);
}// End setup

void loop() {
  digitalWrite(triggerPin, LOW);
  delayMicroseconds(5);
  digitalWrite(triggerPin, HIGH);
  delayMicroseconds(10);
  digitalWrite(triggerPin, LOW);
  Duration = pulseIn(echoSensorPin, HIGH);
  Distance = (Duration /2)/74;
  Serial.print("Distance = ");
  Serial.println(Distance);
  if (Distance < HighWaterDistance) {
   TooHighCount++;
   if (TooHighCount >= MinCount) {
    digitalWrite(DrainPin, HIGH);
    Draining = true;
   }
```

```
  } // End of if (Distance < HighWaterDistance)
  else {
    TooHighCount = 0;
  }
  if (Distance > HighWaterDistance + 1 && Draining) {
    NotTooHighCount++;
    if (NotTooHighCount >= MinCount) {
     digitalWrite(DrainPin, LOW);
     Draining = false;
    }
  } // End of if (Distance > HighWaterDistance + 1)
  else {
    NotTooHighCount = 0;
  }
  if (Distance > LowWaterDistance){
    TooLowCount++;
    if (TooLowCount >= MinCount) {
     digitalWrite(AddWaterPin, HIGH);
     Adding = true;
    }
  } // End of if (Distance > LowWaterDistance
  else {
    TooLowCount = 0;
  }
  if (Distance < LowWaterDistance - 1 && Adding){
    NotTooLowCount++;
     if (NotTooLowCount >= MinCount) {
       digitalWrite(AddWaterPin, LOW);
       Adding = false;
    }
  } // End of if (Distance < LowWaterDistance - 1)
  else {
    NotTooLowCount = 0;
  }
  delay(500);
} //  End main loop
```

Sketch 5.2

Comparing this to Sketch 5.1, we first added the unsigned long variables TooHighCount, NotTooHighCount, TooLowCount, and NotTooLowCount, and assigned them each a value of 0. These are counting variables that will count how many times in a row the water was too high, not too high, too low, and not too low. We added boolean (true or false) variables Draining and Adding and set them to false. These keep track of whether you are currently draining or adding water to the tank. We also add integer variable MinCount and set it to 4. This is the number of readings you want to take before taking action. You can set this to any number you want.

The Setup routine is unchanged from Sketch 5.1, as is the part of the loop routine that actually measures the distance and stores it in the variable Distance. The first part of the actual operation that changes is in the part of the code that is activated when if Distance is less than HighWaterDistance. Instead of immediately setting DrainPin high (turning on the drain), it starts counting. The statement
TooHighCount++;
increases TooHighCount by 1. The statement
if (TooHighCount >= MinCount)
means "if TooHighCount is greater than or equal to MinCount." When this is true, the code sets DrainPin high. It also sets the variable Draining to true, to help keep track of the fact that you are currently draining the water.

If the condition Distance < HighWaterDistance is not true, the else condition resets TooHighCount to 0. This ensures that the count of times in a row that the water level is too high starts at 0 when the water level first becomes too high.

The statement
if (Distance > HighWaterDistance + 1)
from Sketch 5.1 has been changed to
if (Distance > HighWaterDistance + 1 && Draining)

In C, && (two & symbols) means AND, so this if statement means "if Distance is greater than HighWaterDistance +1 and Draining is true." If both of these conditions is true, the statement
NotTooHighCount++;
increases NotTooHighCount by 1. (In the C language, putting a ++ after a variable name means to add 1 to the current value of that variable.) Then the statement
if (NotTooHighCount >= MinCount)
checks to see if NotTooHighCount is greater than or equal to MinCount. If it is,
digitalWrite(DrainPin, LOW);
turns off the draining relay and the variable Draining is set to false again. If the
if (Distance > HighWaterDistance + 1 && Draining)
condition is not met, the else statement is activated and NotTooHighCount is set to 0 to make sure that it starts at 0 the next time the water level drops by 1 inch while the water is draining.

 The same process occurs if the water level drops too low. The
if (Distance > LowWaterDistance)
statement takes effect if the lower level drops too low, or to put it more accurately, if the distance to the top of the water gets too great (greater than LowWaterDistance). The first thing that happens is that the statement
TooLowCount++;
adds 1 to TooLowCount. When this has happened the number of times you set in MinCount, the if statement
if (TooLowCount >= MinCount)
proceeds to the statement that sets AddWaterPin high, activating the pump or valve that you use to add water to your system and also setting the variable Adding to true to store the fact that you are now adding water. If Distance is not greater than LowWaterDistance, the else statement resets the TooLowCount to 0.

 After this, if the distance to the water top is less than LowWaterDistance - 1 (indicating that the water level

has risen an inch) and water is being still being added (shown by Adding being true), the statement NotTooLowCount++;
increases the count NotTooLowCount by 1. Once this reaches MinCount, the AddWaterPin is set to low, turning off the water flow to the tank, and Adding is set to false. If the distance to the top of the ware is not less than LowWaterDistance - 1 or Adding is not true, the else statement sets NotTooLowCount to 0.

That is the end of the tests. There is then a 500 millisecond (1/2 second) delay to let things settle before the loop repeats.

If you do not want to use the ultrasonic sensor, you can simply place a sensor in the tank that will trigger when the water reaches it. This will not tell you the actual water level, but only yes or no whether the water is at or above a certain level. The simplest way to test this is with a float switch, such as the one shown in Figures 5.4 and 5.5.

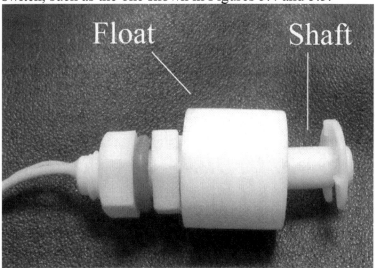

Figure 5.4

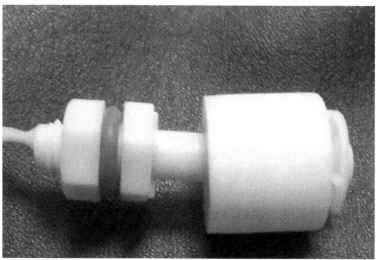

Figure 5.5

The float switch is placed in the water with the wire end up. Above water, the float portion will fall to the bottom of the shaft, as seen in Figure 5.5. When water rises so that the float portion is under water, it floats up to the top of the shaft in the position shown in Figure 5.4. When the float is at the top of the shaft, the switch is open (off). When it falls to the bottom, the switch closes and current can flow through the switch. You can put two in the water if you want, one at the highest level you want the water to go to and one at the lowest level. Connect one wire from each one to the Arduino GND pin, and the other wire of each to a different digital input pin on the Arduino. Sketch 5.3 will control draining and adding water with two sensors arranged this way. This sketch assumes that you have connected the drain relay to pin 13, the add water relay to pin 12, the wire from the higher float switch to pin 11, and the wire from the lower float switch to pin 10.

```
#define DrainPin 13
#define AddWaterPin 12
#define HighWaterPin 11
#define LowWaterPin 10
```

```
int HighWater;
int LowWater;

void setup(){
  pinMode(LowWaterPin, INPUT_PULLUP);
  pinMode(HighWaterPin, INPUT_PULLUP);
  pinMode(DrainPin, OUTPUT);
  digitalWrite(DrainPin, LOW);
  pinMode(AddWaterPin, OUTPUT);
  digitalWrite(AddWaterPin, LOW);
}// End setup

void loop() {
  HighWater = digitalRead(HighWaterPin);
  LowWater = digitalRead(LowWaterPin);
  if (HighWater == HIGH) {
    digitalWrite(DrainPin, HIGH);
  }
  else {
    digitalWrite(DrainPin, LOW);
  }
  if (LowWater == LOW) {
    digitalWrite(AddWaterPin, HIGH);
  }
  else {
    digitalWrite(AddWaterPin, LOW);
  }
} // End main loop
```
                        Sketch 5.3

First, we define which four pins we will be using for input and output. We also initialize two variables, HighWater and LowWater. These will store whether the two input pins are high or low, which indicate if the water is too high or too low, respectively. The setup routine sets the pin mode (input or output) for each of four pins, and sets the two output pins to initially low (off). The lines

pinMode(LowWaterPin, INPUT_PULLUP);
pinMode(HighWaterPin, INPUT_PULLUP);
set the two digital pins LowWaterPin and HighWaterPin to input mode, but they also do something else. The value INPUT_PULLUP tells the pin to be an input but also internally connect a pull-up resistor inside the Arduino to the pin. This applies a weak (low current) 5 volts to it, which will cause it to read high, unless you are applying a stronger ground connection to it. Of course, that is exactly what you are doing when the switch closes and connects the pin to ground. Therefore, each of the two input pins reads high until the switch closes (turns on).

In the loop routine, the lines
HighWater = digitalRead(HighWaterPin);
LowWater = digitalRead(LowWaterPin);
use the digitalRead function to read the two input pins and store the results in the variables HighWater and LowWater. Then you have the statement
if (HighWater == HIGH)
which tests to see if the vale of HighWater is HIGH. HIGH is a built-in constant that equals 1. It is important to notice that there are two equal signs in this statement. In C, one equal sign assigns a value and two together tests the value. For example, X = 1 would set the variable X to the value 1, while X == 1 tests to see if X equals 1.

If HighWater has a value of 1 (HIGH), the pin called DrainPin is set high (turned on), activating whatever you are using to drain water. If HighWater is not HIGH, the drain pin is turned off.

Next, if LowWater is LOW (0), the AddWaterPin pin is set HIGH, turning on the pump or valve to add water. If LowWater is not LOW, the else statement turns off the add water pump or valve to stop adding water. Notice that the test for HighWater is the opposite as the test for LowWater. This code turns DrainPin on if HighWater is HIGH, but turns AddWaterPin on if LowWater is LOW. Remember that the float switch turns on, connecting the pin it is attached to ground, if it is out of the water. We want

DrainPin to turn on if the water has reached a level where the upper float switch is under water, but we want AddWaterPin to turn on if the lower switch is NOT under water.

This is a very simple sketch, and it does drain the water if the water gets too high and add water if it gets too low. There is one small problem. It turns off the drain the moment the water drops just below the too high water level and turns off adding water as soon as the water gets just above the low water level. This can cause the valves or pumps to go on and off frequently as the water level fluctuates near the high or low levels, even in response to ripples in the water from wind or fish movements. Having a pump or valve turn on and off frequently can result in unnecessary wear. It might be preferable to have the water drain a little below the high water level and rise a little above the low water level before turning off the pump or valve.

There are several ways to do this. One would be to have additional water level detectors. You could have one just below the high water level detector to turn off the drain when the water got below that and one just above the low water detector to turn off adding water when it got to that. Sketch 5.4 shows how to do this, with the float switch just below the high water switch connected to pin 9 and the float switch just above the low water switch connected to pin 8.

```
#define DrainPin 13
#define AddWaterPin 12
#define HighWaterPin 11
#define LowWaterPin 10
#define NotHighWaterPin 9
#define NotLowWaterPin 8

int HighWater;
int LowWater;
int NotHighWater;
```

```
int NotLowWater;

void setup(){
  pinMode(LowWaterPin, INPUT_PULLUP);
  pinMode(HighWaterPin, INPUT_PULLUP);
  pinMode(DrainPin, OUTPUT);
  digitalWrite(DrainPin, LOW);
  pinMode(AddWaterPin, OUTPUT);
  digitalWrite(AddWaterPin, LOW);
}// End setup

void loop() {
  HighWater = digitalRead(HighWaterPin);
  LowWater = digitalRead(LowWaterPin);
  NotHighWater = digitalRead(NotHighWaterPin);
  NotLowWater = digitalRead(NotLowWaterPin);
  if (HighWater == HIGH) {
    digitalWrite(DrainPin, HIGH);
  }
  if (NotHighWater == LOW) {
    digitalWrite(DrainPin, LOW);
  }
  if (LowWater == LOW) {
    digitalWrite(AddWaterPin, HIGH);
  }
  if (NotLowWater == HIGH) {
    digitalWrite(AddWaterPin, LOW);
  }
} // End main loop
```
Sketch 5.4

This could be rather burdensome, however, requiring you to mount two more float switches and using two more of the pins on the Arduino. A simpler method is just to add a small delay after the pump or valve is turned on to drain or add water. Sketch 5.5 shows how to do this.

```
#define DrainPin 13
```

```
#define AddWaterPin 12
#define HighWaterPin 11
#define LowWaterPin 10

// Delay times in seconds
unsigned long DrainTime = 15;
unsigned long AddTime = 30;

int HighWater;
int LowWater;
unsigned long currentTime;
unsigned long HighEndTime;
unsigned long LowEndTime;

void setup(){
  pinMode(LowWaterPin, INPUT_PULLUP);
  pinMode(HighWaterPin, INPUT_PULLUP);
  pinMode(DrainPin, OUTPUT);
  digitalWrite(DrainPin, LOW);
  pinMode(AddWaterPin, OUTPUT);
  digitalWrite(AddWaterPin, LOW);
}// End setup

void loop() {
  HighWater = digitalRead(HighWaterPin);
  LowWater = digitalRead(LowWaterPin);
  currentTime = millis();
  if (HighWater == HIGH) {
   digitalWrite(DrainPin, HIGH);
   HighEndTime = currentTime;
  }
  else {
   if (currentTime - HighEndTime > DrainTime * 1000 ||
HighEndTime > currentTime) {
     digitalWrite(DrainPin, LOW);
   }
  }
  if (LowWater == LOW) {
```

```
    digitalWrite(AddWaterPin, HIGH);
    LowEndTime = currentTime;
  }
  else {
    if (currentTime - LowEndTime > AddTime * 1000 || LowEndTime > currentTime) {
      digitalWrite(AddWaterPin, LOW);
    }
  }
} // End main loop
```

Sketch 5.5

This is Sketch 5.3 with some additions. The lines
unsigned long DrainTime = 15;
unsigned long AddTime = 30;
define the variables DrainTime and AddTime that allow you to set how many seconds to drain or add water. This will drain water for 15 seconds after the water level drops below the maximum and add water for 30 seconds after the water rises above the minimum. You can change these to whatever you want. The proper times will depend on the size of your water tank and how much margin you want between the limits and the water level.

The line
currentTime = millis();
records the current time since the Arduino started running in the variable currentTime. If the water is too high, the line
HighEndTime = currentTime;
stores this in HighEndTime. It will continue to do this as long as the water level is too high, and stop when the water goes below this level. Thus, HighEndTime stores the end of the time that the water level was too high. If the water level is below the high water level, the else statement is executed. The if statement

if (currentTime - HighEndTime > DrainTime * 1000 || HighEndTime > currentTime) checks to see if the time between the current time and the last recorded HighEndTime is greater than you chosen DrainTime. (The "* 1000" converts your seconds into milliseconds.) If so, DrainPin is set low and the draining stops. Notice that in the if statement there is also || HighEndTime > currentTime. The || means OR in C. The | symbol is the one above the \ symbol on your keyboard. That is, | is what you get when you hold down the Shift key and press the \ key. Thus, || HighEndTime > currentTime mean "or HighEndTime is greater than the current time." Remember our discussion of rollover of the millis() function. In the extremely unlikely event that millis() rolls over while your water is draining, currentTime would become less than HighEndTime and the condition currentTime - HighEndTime > DrainTime * 1000 would never be satisfied. The water would continue draining indefinitely. Although the odds against this happening are astronomically high, the results of continued draining would be so disastrous that I have provided this alternative condition for shutting off the draining. If rollover occurred during draining, HighEndTime would greater than the current time and the draining would stop.

The same procedure is used for adding water. While water is being added, LowEndTime is constantly being set to currentTime. Once the water level is above the minimum level, this stops, so LowEndTime records the time the water was last too low. The else statement then is activated. The statement

if (currentTime - LowEndTime > AddTime * 1000 || LowEndTime > currentTime)

checks to see if the current time minus LowEndTime is greater than the time you set to add water. If so,
digitalWrite(AddWaterPin, LOW);
turns off the drain relay. Again, I have added the condition || LowEndTime > currentTime (meaning "OR

LowEndTime is greater than the current time"), so that if rollover has occurred while water is being added the water adding is shut off.

There is one other point worth mentioning. I explained INPUT_PULLUP, which adds an internal pull-up resistor to ensure that the input reads HIGH when the float switch is not connecting it to ground. I have found that in some of the cheaper Arduino knockoffs, this internal pull-up resistor does not work well. The input may read LOW even if the switch is turned off. If this happens, you should add an external pull-up resistor between the 5 volt pin and the input pin. A 10 K or 20 K resistor works well for this. Figure 5.6 shows the circuit, including relays, switches, and resistors. If you have a good Arduino and do not need the external resistors, you can omit them.

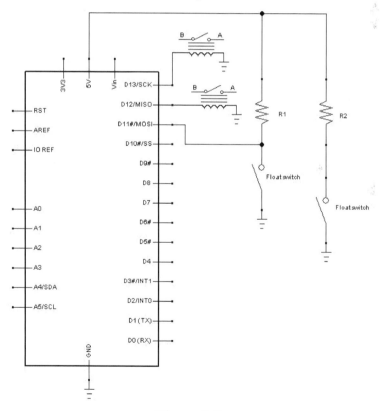

Figure 5.6

Another type of sensor that an be used to detect water levels is shown in Figure 5.7.

Figure 5.7

As you can see, it has three connector pins, for V+, GND, and analog output (marked S). It also has rows of wires, with alternate wires being connected. When the sensor gets wet, current is conducted between each alternate wire, causing the voltage at the output pin to go up. This can be placed so that water will contact the lower part (to the right in Figure 5.7), so that when the water reaches the sensor it makes the electrical contact. This type of sensor is not good for detecting low water levels, because if it is totally submerged, water can short out or damage the electronic components. However, it can be useful for detecting when water has reached a high level. This is not the best sensor in most situations because of this, but it can be useful in some situations. It can be used for detecting water in gravel beds. The reason for this is that the previous two types of sensors will not work well there. The ultrasonic sensor will detect the gravel, and the gravel may interfere with the movement of the float in the float sensor if you put that in the gravel. An additional use for this sensor is to place it flat on the floor near water tanks as a leakage or spillage detector, since it will detect very low levels of water spilled on it when it is lying flat, unlike the other sensors.

The analog reading when the sensor is dry is 0. In my tests, the analog reading shot up to about 400 as soon as the water covers the bottom of the sensor even 2 mm deep. Totally immersing it raised the reading to about 540. After removing the sensor from the water, enough water clung to the sensor to keep the reading at about 250. A single drop lying across any two wires will keep a reading in the hundreds. Since this is based on how much current is conducted, the readings will also be influenced by the conductivity of the water. For example, if you have minerals in the water, the reading will go up at the same level of water.

Since this is an analog output, you need to use an analog input on the Arduino. Sketch 5.6 shows how to do this.

```
#define RelayPin 13
 int Triggerpoint = 200;
 int Reading;

void setup() {
  // put your setup code here, to run once:
   pinMode(RelayPin, OUTPUT);
   digitalWrite(RelayPin, LOW );
}

void loop() {
  // put your main code here, to run repeatedly:
  Reading = analogRead(A1);
  if (Reading > Triggerpoint) {
    digitalWrite(RelayPin, HIGH);
  }
  else {
    digitalWrite(RelayPin, LOW);
  }
}
```

Sketch 5.6

The relay pin that takes action if water is detected is defined as 13. An arbitrary analog input level of 200 is set. The exact value does not matter much, since the level is 0 when the sensor is dry. You just want to be sure that the trigger level is between 0 and the level that you will get once the water reaches the sensor. The integer variable Reading is the reading you will get from the analog input. The Setup routine merely defines the digital output pin as output and sets it initially to LOW. Notice that you do not have to define the analog pin. Analog pins are input by default.

In the loop routine, the line
Reading = analogRead(A1);
reads analog input A1 and stores the value in the variable Reading. Then the
if (Reading > Triggerpoint)
statement sets the relay pin high, turning on the relay, and the else statement turns it back off when the reading goes back down below the trigger point.

I will not elaborate more on this sensor. Most of the previous discussions of the other sensors apply to this sensor. You can add time delays to turning off the relay or other features from the previous sketches if you like.

Chapter 6

Moisture Levels in Soil

It might seem strange to have a chapter on measuring moisture levels in soil in a book about aquaponics and hydroponics. Don't those terms mean growing food without soil? However, even in hydroponics, you sometimes grow some plants in soil. You sometimes need to grow the plants in soil to get them started before you transfer them to water. Some people consider vertical gardening, which can use pots of soil, to be a form of hydroponics. You may need to use soil for some root vegetables, and water them with water from your fish tanks. If you do, you will probably want to water them automatically by having a pump turn on or a valve open to water the soil. One way is a timer, but that would not account for factors like heat and humidity that can affect how fast the soil dries out. You can use the timer from Chapter 3 that allows for that, but you can also test the soil directly.

To test the soil moister level, you can use a commercially available probe like the one in Figure 6.1.

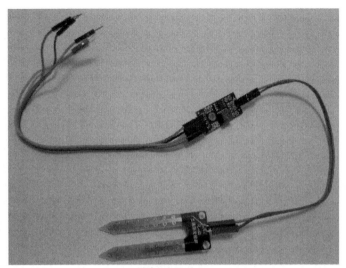
Figure 6.1

These measure the moisture in the soil by passing a very weak electrical current through the soil and measuring the resistance. However, I do not recommend these. For one thing, they seem to be rather unreliable. They often give widely varying results. More importantly, the metal contacts are a very thin layer on plastic. They tend to corrode away very quickly. I have even read reports of the metal dissolving in a matter of days. There are some that work by capacitance rather than resistance, which prevents the corrosion. However, these cost more. One problem that I think can be significant in all of these is that they measure the moisture in a very small area, between or immediately around the probe. If that area is particularly wet or dry, you can get misleading readings.

I suggest making your own. All you need is two pieces of metal and a resistor. Just drive the two pieces of metal into the soil at opposite ends of a flower pot or other container. This will measure the resistance of the entire container, not just one small area. For the metal, almost anything will do. I have tried a pair of 3" nails, and found them to work well. Of course, these will rust out rather quickly and need to be either replaced or sanded off. A more durable choice would be something like aluminum baking nails, stainless steel covered nails, or any corrosion resistant metal spikes. Before inserting the nails into the soil, wrap the end of a wire around the metal spikes tightly and repeatedly to make a good electrical contact. If you can solder the wires onto the metal, that is even better. Anything to improve the electrical contact between the wires and the metal spikes will help. Figure 6.2 shows the setup.

Figure 6.2

Connect one of the wires to an Arduino digital output, such as D2, and one to an analog input, such as A0. Connect a resistor from that analog input to another digital output, such as D3. The exact value of the resistor does not matter. Ideally, the best value would be about the same resistance as the pot has when the moisture level is just too low, but this is not critical. I find that about 1 K to 2.2 K usually works best, but it will depend on the size of the pot, the type of soil, and how dry you want the soil to get before you water it. Figure 6.3 shows this as a schematic. With this circuit, the drier the soil is, the higher the reading at the analog input will be. If the soil is completely dry, the reading will be 1023 (or 4095 if your Arduino uses that scale). If the soil is very wet, it will be in the low hundreds.

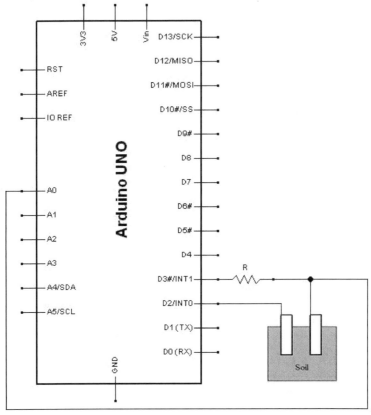

Figure 6.3

You can actually put several pots in series, rather than just one, as shown in Figure 6.4. This will cause a high analog reading if any one of the pots goes dry.

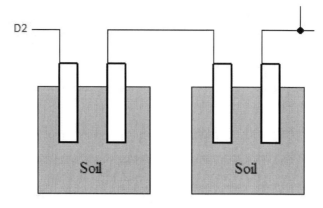

Figure 6.4

The reason for connecting the soil sensor and the resistor to the digital output pins is that this allows you to turn off the current, and even reverse it. There are several problems with running a continuous current through the soil. Aside from the continuous power drain, it can cause the metal connected to a positive connection to dissolve. It can also build up a slight charge in the soil around the electrodes that can cause the readings to become inaccurate because this charge opposes the current flow. You can avoid these problems if you apply power to the soil sensor only briefly while you want to take a reading, and then reverse the current for the same amount of time. Sketch 6.1 does this.

```
#define AddWaterPin 13
#define PowerPin1 3
#define PowerPin2 2

// Analog reading when soil is too dry
int TooDry = 600;
// Number of seconds to water the plant
unsigned long WaterTime = 30;
// Number of seconds between tests (300 = 5 minutes)
unsigned long TestInterval = 300;
unsigned long LastTest = 0;
```

```
bool WaterOn = false;
int MoistureLevel;
unsigned long StartTime;
unsigned long currentTime;

// Need changes starting here
void setup(){
  pinMode(AddWaterPin, OUTPUT);
  digitalWrite(AddWaterPin, LOW );
  pinMode(PowerPin1, OUTPUT);
  digitalWrite(PowerPin1, LOW );
  pinMode(PowerPin2, OUTPUT);
  digitalWrite(PowerPin2, LOW );
  Serial.begin(9600);
}// End setup

void loop() {
  currentTime = millis();
  if (LastTest > currentTime) {
    LastTest = 0;
  }
  if (currentTime - LastTest > TestInterval * 1000) {
    digitalWrite(PowerPin1, HIGH);
    delay(500);
    MoistureLevel = analogRead(A0);
    digitalWrite(PowerPin1, LOW);
    digitalWrite(PowerPin2, HIGH);
    delay(500);
    digitalWrite(PowerPin2, LOW);
    Serial.print("Moisture = ");
    Serial.println(MoistureLevel);
    if (MoistureLevel > TooDry) {
      digitalWrite(AddWaterPin, HIGH);
      StartTime = currentTime;
      WaterOn = true;
    }
    LastTest = currentTime;
  }
```

```
  if (WaterOn) {
    if (StartTime > currentTime) {
      StartTime = 0;
    }
    if (currentTime - StartTime > WaterTime * 1000) {
      digitalWrite(AddWaterPin, LOW);
      WaterOn = false;
    }
  }
} // End main loop
```

Sketch 6.1

First, you define the AddWaterPin, the pin to the relay that will turn on a pump or valve to add water, as pin 13. We also define the two power pins that will control power to the sensor. Next, you set the integer variable TooDry. This is the analog reading you want to trigger watering the plants. Next, you set WaterTime. This is the amount of time, in seconds, you want the plants to be watered once watering starts. This is necessary because once water starts pouring into the pot, it will probably pool on top the soil, making a direct connection between your metal spikes. You do not want watering to cut off as soon as this happens. You want the watering to continue for some period of time so that the soil will get thoroughly soaked. TestInterval is the period of time between tests of the soil moisture, measured in seconds. I have set it to 300 seconds, which is 5 minutes, but you can set it to any value you want. LastTest is the time of the most recent test, and should be initialized at 0. WaterOn records whether the water is currently on (plants being watered).

The setup section simply defines the AddWaterPin, PowerPin1, and PowerPin2 as output and sets them low (off) to start. It also activates serial communication so the Arduino can send information to your computer.

In the loop routine, it first sets currentTime to the current time, measured as milliseconds since the Arduino was turned on. The
if (LastTest > currentTime)
test checks to see if the millis() function has rolled over, as discussed in previous chapters. The test
if (currentTime - LastTest > TestInterval * 1000)
then tests to see if the current time minus the last time the test was conducted is greater than the time interval you set. The "* 1000" is used to convert the time interval to milliseconds, since the other numbers are in milliseconds.

If the desired time interval has passed, the next line sets PowerPin1 HIGH (5 volts) to power the sensor. The delay of 500 milliseconds is to make sure the power pin is fully powered up and current is flowing. This is probably unnecessary, but it does not hurt to give it a half second to stabilize. The next line reads the A0 analog pin with the function analogRead(A0) and stores this information in the variable MoistureLevel. Once the reading is taken, the next three lines reverse the current flow and then delay for the same period of time (500 milliseconds). As explained previously, this prevents any electrical charge from building up and may also help recapture some metal ions that may have been released from the metal sensor when it became positively charged. The next line turns off the power, so both metal rods are at ground and no current is flowing. The Serial.print commands send this reading to your computer to let you monitor the moisture levels if you like.

If the analog reading is greater than the TooDry level you have set, the
if (MoistureLevel > TooDry)
statement turns on the relay that turns on the pump or valve to water the soil, using the command
digitalWrite(AddWaterPin, HIGH);
It also sets StartTime, the time when watering starts, to the current time, and sets WaterOn to true to indicate that water is flowing.

Regardless of whether the water is turned on, the line LastTest = currentTime sets the time of this test to the current time. This is necessary to allow the next test to be the desired time interval after this test.

Once water is flowing, the statement
if (WaterOn)
takes effect. This is the part of the code that leaves the water on for the desired period of time. Remember that StartTime is set to when watering starts. First, we have the familiar
if (StartTime > currentTime)
code that resets StartTime in case millis() has rolled over. Then we have the
if (currentTime - StartTime > WaterTime * 1000)
statement that checks to see if the time since StartTime is greater than the watering time period. If the current time minus the time the watering starting is greater than the time you specified to continue the watering (the 1000 converts milliseconds to seconds), this condition is satisfied. If this condition is met, the statement
digitalWrite(AddWaterPin, LOW);
turns off the watering. WaterOn is set to false, since the watering has stopped.

The biggest problem with this is that you have to decide what value to set for TooDry. To set this, you need to know what the analog reading will be when the soil is dry enough to start watering again. One way to do this is to monitor the soil manually and wait for the soil to get dry enough. When this happens, plug the Arduino into your computer with the USB connector, run the Arduino IDE, and run the serial monitor. Because of the Serial.print statements in the code, the serial monitor will be showing you the analog reading. Write this down, then change the TooDry value in the code and reload the sketch into the Arduino.

A simpler way is to have the Arduino set and record the correct TooDry value when the soil reaches the proper level of dryness to start watering. You can have the

Arduino do this when you briefly connect one input pin to GND. To do this, use Sketch 6.2.

```
#include <EEPROM.h>

#define AddWaterPin 13
#define SetPin 12
#define PowerPin1 3
#define PowerPin2 2

// Analog reading when soil is too dry
int TooDry = 5000;
// Number of seconds to water the plant
unsigned long WaterTime = 30;
// Number of seconds between tests (300 = 5 minutes)
unsigned long TestInterval = 300;
unsigned long LastTest = 0;
bool WaterOn = false;
int MoistureLevel;
unsigned long StartTime;
unsigned long currentTime;

void setup(){
  pinMode(AddWaterPin, OUTPUT);
  digitalWrite(AddWaterPin, LOW );
  pinMode(SetPin, INPUT_PULLUP);
  pinMode(PowerPin1, OUTPUT);
  digitalWrite(PowerPin1, LOW );
  pinMode(PowerPin2, OUTPUT);
  digitalWrite(PowerPin2, LOW );
  Serial.begin(9600);
  if (EEPROM.read(2) == 11){
    Serial.println("Loading TooDry");
    byte high = EEPROM.read(0);
    byte low =  EEPROM.read(1);
    TooDry = (high << 8) + low;
    Serial.print("TooDry = ");
    Serial.println(TooDry);
```

```
  }
}// End setup

void loop() {
  currentTime = millis();
  if (LastTest > currentTime) {
    LastTest = 0;
  }
  if (digitalRead(SetPin) == LOW) {
    GetReading();
    TooDry = MoistureLevel;
    EEPROM.write(0, highByte(TooDry));
    EEPROM.write(1, lowByte(TooDry));
    EEPROM.write(2, 11);
    Serial.print("Too dry level set");
  }
  if (currentTime - LastTest > TestInterval * 1000) {
    GetReading();
    if (MoistureLevel > TooDry) {
      digitalWrite(AddWaterPin, HIGH);
      StartTime = currentTime;
      WaterOn = true;
    }
    LastTest = currentTime;
  }
  if (WaterOn) {
    if (StartTime > currentTime) {
      StartTime = 0;
    }
    if (currentTime - StartTime > WaterTime * 1000) {
      digitalWrite(AddWaterPin, LOW);
      WaterOn = false;
    }
  }
} // End main loop

void GetReading(){
  digitalWrite(PowerPin1, HIGH);
```

```
    delay(500);
    MoistureLevel = analogRead(A0);
    digitalWrite(PowerPin1, LOW);
    digitalWrite(PowerPin2, HIGH);
    delay(500);
    digitalWrite(PowerPin2, LOW);
    Serial.print("Moisture = ");
    Serial.println(MoistureLevel);
}
```

Sketch 6.2

This is Sketch 6.1 with some additions. First, we have included the library EEPROM.h, which has functions that let you store data in the Arduino's permanent memory. When the Arduino loses power, the code is retained in permanent memory but the value of variables is lost. However, it is possible to store data in the same type of memory as the code, as will be demonstrated by this sketch. You do not have to install the EEPROM.h library on your computer, because it is included with the IDE.

We have also defined SetPin as 12. This is the pin that you will briefly connect to ground to store the TooDry level. (You can use a different pin if you like.) I have also changed the initial TooDry value to 5000. This is beyond the maximum value, and it will prevent the relay from being activated until you set the proper TooDry level.

I have put the code that tests the soil moisture in a subroutine called GetReading. This is because the reading will now be taken from two parts of the code. It will be taken by the normal process used in Sketch 6.1, when the preset time interval occurs to test the moisture, but it will also be called to get the level when you are setting the TooDry variable. Putting the nine lines of code involved in testing the moisture level into a subroutine instead of simply typing it twice saves space in memory, makes the code easier to read, and makes it easier to change. For example, if you decided to change the delay times you would only have to change them once instead of searching the code to make sure you change them everywhere.

  I will skip over the setup routine for a moment and get to the loop routine. The first addition is the statement
if (digitalRead(SetPin) == LOW)
This detects when you have connected pin 12 to ground. When this happens, the GetReading() subroutine is called to get the MoistureLevel value. When the code returns from the subroutine, TooDry is set equal to the current value of MoistureLevel. This repeats as long as pin 12 is connected to ground. Once you disconnect pin 12 from ground, TooDry will retain the last value it had before you disconnected pin 12. However, normally it would lose this value when the Arduino loses power. The lines
EEPROM.write(0, highByte(TooDry));
EEPROM.write(1, lowByte(TooDry));
store the value of TooDry in the permanent memory on locations 0 and 1. It is necessary to do this in two steps because one byte of memory is only big enough to store half the value of an integer, so the integer is broken up into two parts, high and low (no relation to the HIGH and LOW values of pins). If you do not understand all this technical jargon, don't worry about it. It is not necessary for you to understand this part to use this sketch.

  The line
EEPROM.write(2, 11);
stores the value of 11 in memory location 2. There is no particular significance to the value 11. It could have been any number from 1 to 253. The only purpose of storing a particular number in location 3 is to signal that the value of TooDry has been stored, as will be explained in the next paragraph.

  Now we go back to the setup routine. Here we add the test
if (EEPROM.read(2) == 11)
Notice again the double equal sign, indicating a test of whether the two values are equal, not setting them equal. The function EEPROM.read(2) reads the value of memory

location 2. If this equals 11, this indicates that the value of TooDry has been saved during a previous run of the Arduino. If so, the lines

byte high = EEPROM.read(0);
byte low = EEPROM.read(1);
TooDry = (high << 8) + low;

read the data stored in memory locations 0 and 1, convert the two bytes of data back into an integer value, and store it in TooDry. Thus, when the Arduino is powered up, if during a previous run you had stored a value for TooDry, that value is now used. Otherwise, TooDry retains the value of 5000 set for it earlier.

You now have a simple way to configure the Arduino with the proper analog value to start watering the plants. Just run the Arduino with the probes in the pot(s). When you find that the soil is almost dry enough to add water, connect the pin 12 to GND momentarily and then disconnect it again immediately. You can actually connect pin 12 to the 5V pin if you want, to make sure that pin 12 stays HIGH and does not reset later. This should be unnecessary because the internal pull-up resistor should keep it high, but in some cheaper Arduinos this resistor is not very good, and some random static electricity or interference might conceivably cause a brief negative pulse. Best to be completely safe by connecting the set pin to 5V.

Note that the sketch actually starts the water when the soil is drier than TooDry, not exactly at that level, so water will not start flowing until it gets just a little drier. The difference should be very small, but just to be safe you should set the TooDry level just before the soil really needs watering by connecting the set pin to ground then.

Chapter 7

Testing and Controlling pH

One of the most important and things to keep track of in an aquaponic/hydroponic system is the pH of the water. This can be done by titration, where a chemical is added to the water until a visible chemical reaction, like a color change, occurs which indicates the pH. It can be done with test strips that change color based on pH. It can also be done by putting an electronic probe into the water. This latter method lends itself well to electronic monitoring and automation.

There are several models of electronic probes commercially available that are specifically designed to be connected to Arduinos. These have a probe that goes into the water and connects by wire to a circuit board. The circuit board is then connected to the Arduino. Figure 7.1 shows one of these.

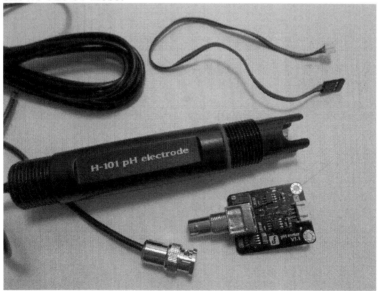

Figure 7.1

This shows the pH Sensor / Meter Pro Kit for Arduino version SEN0169 sold by DFRobot. This is the one I recommend. It is a bit more expensive ($56.96 + shipping at the time this book was written), but it is advertised to last up to two years in use. This Pro version is designed to be able to be used continuously. Do not purchase the DFRobot version SEN0161, the blue probe. That one is for laboratory use and is not rated for continuous use. The DFRobot pH probe comes with a circuit board that the probe plugs into, as shown in Figure 7.1. This has a connector at the other side of the circuit board from the probe connect. A plug comes with the circuit board that connects to this and has three wires, red, black and blue. The red wire connects to the Arduino 5V, the black to GND, and the blue to an analog input. These wires have female connectors, so you will need to use male/male connector cables or 22 to 24 gauge single core wire to connect these to the Arduino.

Another model of probe is shown in Figure 7.2. This model is much cheaper (you can get it for under $7.00 from China on eBay), but I have not found specs for its durability. It does appear to work satisfactorily in my tests.

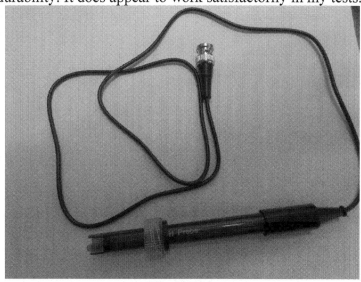

Figure 7.2

If you are using a probe that does not come with the circuit board, you need to buy the board. I have found two makes. The first is shown in Figure 7.3.

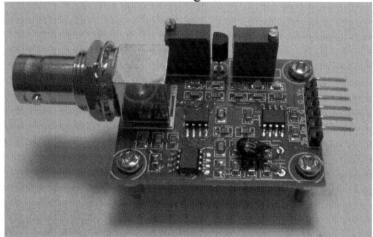

Figure 7.3

There are five pins, which you will connect to the Arduino with male/female cables. The V+ pin goes to Arduino 5V and the G pin next to it goes to GND. The Po pin goes to the Arduino analog input. The To and Do pins are for other outputs that give temperature data for probes that include temperature sensors. One unusual feature of this board is that the output is inverted. For most board, voltage output goes up from 0 to 5 volts as pH goes up. For this one, the output goes down as pH goes up. This requires a software correction that I will explain when I describe the sketches.

Another circuit board is shown in Figure 7.4. I do not recommend this board. It has three pins, 5V power input closest to the sensor probe connector (top pin in picture), the analog output, and the GND connection closest to the edge of the board. In my tests, the output switches back and forth about once per second between a voltage that indicates pH and one that indicates something else (probably ORP). Other than the fact that the other voltage is higher than pH voltage for most normal ranges of pH, there seems to be no way of knowing at any given instant which reading you are getting.

Figure 7.4

For the board in Figure 7.1, the analog output is supposed to vary linearly from 0 to 5 volts, where 0 volts indicates a pH of 0 and 5 volts indicates a pH of 14. For example, a pH of 7 would be indicated by 2.5 volts. For the board in Figure 7.3, 0 volts would indicate a pH of 14 and 5 volts a pH of 0. Unfortunately, these do not work as well as they are supposed to. The output can often be nonlinear, so that the output does not correctly correspond to the pH. It is necessary to calibrate the meter. Many of the circuit boards have one or more potentiometers on them that you are supposed to adjust manually while dipping the probe in a solution with a known pH. You are supposed to dip the probe into a solutions of pH 4 and adjust the potentiometers until the output is correct on the linear scale for that pH. Then you are supposed to rinse off the probe in clean water and dip it in a solution with a different pH, usually 6.8, 7, or 9.2 and repeat the process with the other potentiometer. However, when you adjust the second potentiometer, it alters the reading for a pH of 4. Readjusting the first potentiometer while the probe is back in the pH 4 solution then messes up the reading for the higher pH, and so on. Even then, you do not get a good linear scale for most pH values. All told, quite frustrating.

I have found that a better solution is to have the software perform calculations that compensate for the inaccuracies of the supposedly linear scale. I have devised code (Sketch 7.1) that allow you to calibrate the readings based on three calibrations.

In order to do this, you need to prepare three calibration solutions with low, medium (around 6.8 or 7), and high pH. Packages to make these solutions are readily available on Amazon.com or eBay for performing the less successful hardware calibrations. Figure 7.5 shows the packages for preparing solutions of pH 4.0, 6.8, and 9.2. The packages are usually sold in this combination. You can also buy premixed solutions, but finding all three is hard.

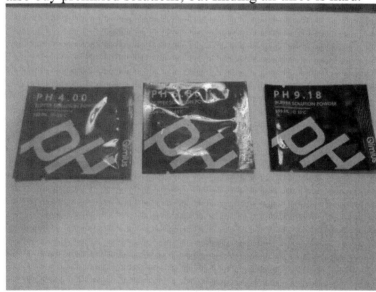

Figure 7.5

Just mix each packet into a separate container of water, preferably distilled or at least filtered. Each packet is usually designed to be mixed with one cup of water, but check the instructions to be sure.

Download the sketch onto the Arduino with the probe connected. Also run the serial monitor. You are definitely going to need it. I mentioned that the serial monitor can display text sent from the Arduino. The serial monitor also has a small text box at the top where you can send text messages to the Arduino. You will use this during the calibration.

Once you have the sketch loaded and the serial monitor running and receiving messages from the Arduino, dip the probe in a low pH solution. You will see pH readings displayed on the Serial monitor. Do not be alarmed if these are far from the pH value of your solution since the software is not calibrated yet. Once these stabilize to a fairly consistent value, type CL (short for calibrate low) followed by the pH value of your solution in the serial monitor text box and press the Enter key or click on the Send button on the serial monitor. For example, for a pH solution of 4, type CL4 in the serial monitor text box and press Enter.

Next, wash off the probe with clean water and dip it into the high pH solution, such as 9.2. The readings on the serial monitor should increase, although not necessarily to 9.2. Once the readings have stabilized, type CU (for calibrate upper) followed by the pH of your solution (such as CU9.2) in the text box and press enter. At this point, the readings for the pH in the serial monitor should be pretty close to the pH of your solution.

Next, wash off the probe in clean water and put it into the medium pH solution. Once the readings stabilize, type CM (for calibrate medium) followed by the pH of your medium solution (such as CM6.8) in the text box and press Enter. The Arduino is now calibrated. The values are stored in nonvolatile memory, just like the trigger levels for watering your plants were in the previous chapter, so you do not have to repeat this process when you disconnect the Arduino from power.

You should find that you can put the probe into each of the solutions and get a reading very close to the pH of your solutions. They may be a little off. The probes themselves are usually accurate to within about .1, and readings can drift a bit.

Now, let's get to the sketches. We start out with a sketch (Sketch 7.1) that simply turns on one relay if the pH goes too low and another if it gets too high. This can be used to turn on a light, bell, or other warning signal that you need to check your pH. (I do recommend manually checking the pH to see exactly what the condition is before you take action.)

```
#include <EEPROM.h>

#define LowpHPin 2
#define HighpHPin 3
#define TurnOffSensorPin 4
#define pHInputPin A2
float TooLow = 6.7;
float TooHigh = 7.1;
float PHReading;
float PHReading1;
float PHReading2;
float PHReading3;
int AV;

String CalCommand;
unsigned int CalLow = 292;
float CalLowpH = 4;
unsigned int CalMid = 497;
float CalMidpH = 6.8;
unsigned int CalHigh = 672;
float CalHighpH = 9.2;
byte HighByte;
byte LowByte;
byte CalStatus;
unsigned int TempInt;
bool PHEnabled = true;

void setup(){
  pinMode(LowpHPin, OUTPUT);
  digitalWrite(LowpHPin, LOW);
```

```
pinMode(HighpHPin, OUTPUT);
digitalWrite(HighpHPin, LOW);
pinMode(TurnOffSensorPin, OUTPUT);
digitalWrite(TurnOffSensorPin, LOW);
Serial.begin(9600);
CalStatus = EEPROM.read(3);
if (CalStatus > 7) {
 CalStatus = 0;
 EEPROM.write(3, CalStatus);
}
Serial.println(CalStatus);
if ((CalStatus & 1) == 1){
  HighByte = EEPROM.read(4);
  LowByte =  EEPROM.read(5);
  if (HighByte + LowByte < 510) {
   CalLow = (HighByte << 8) + LowByte;
  }
 HighByte = EEPROM.read(6);
 LowByte =  EEPROM.read(7);
 if (HighByte + LowByte < 510) {
   TempInt = (HighByte << 8) + LowByte;
   CalLowpH = TempInt / 100.0;
 }
}
Serial.print("Low pH: ");
Serial.print(CalLow);
Serial.print("   ");
Serial.println(CalLowpH);

if ((CalStatus & 2) == 2){
 HighByte = EEPROM.read(8);
  LowByte =  EEPROM.read(9);
  if (HighByte + LowByte < 510) {
   CalMid = (HighByte << 8) + LowByte;
  }
 HighByte = EEPROM.read(10);
 LowByte =  EEPROM.read(11);
 if (HighByte + LowByte < 510) {
```

```cpp
      TempInt = (HighByte << 8) + LowByte;
      CalMidpH = TempInt / 100.0;
    }
  }
  Serial.print("Mid pH: ");
  Serial.print(CalMid);
  Serial.print("   ");
  Serial.println(CalMidpH);
  if ((CalStatus & 4) == 4){
    HighByte = EEPROM.read(12);
    LowByte =  EEPROM.read(13);
    if (HighByte + LowByte < 510) {
      CalHigh = (HighByte << 8) + LowByte;
    }
    Serial.println(CalHigh);
    HighByte = EEPROM.read(14);
    LowByte =  EEPROM.read(15);
    if (HighByte + LowByte < 510) {
      TempInt = (HighByte << 8) + LowByte;
      CalHighpH = TempInt / 100.0;
    }
  }
  Serial.print("High pH: ");
  Serial.print(CalHigh);
  Serial.print("   ");
  Serial.println(CalHighpH);
}//  End setup

void loop() {
  if (PHEnabled) {
      digitalWrite(TurnOffSensorPin, LOW);
      while (Serial.available()) {
      delay(4);  //delay to allow buffer to fill
      if (Serial.available() >0) {
        char c = Serial.read();   //gets one byte from serial buffer
        CalCommand += c; // Add bytes to string
      }
```

```
} //End of while loop that reads string
if (CalCommand.length() >0 ){
 CalCommand.toUpperCase();
 Serial.println(CalCommand);
 if (CalCommand.startsWith("CL")) {
  CalCommand = CalCommand.substring(2);
  CalLowpH = CalCommand.toFloat();
  CalLow = GetMiddleAnalog();
  CalStatus = CalStatus | 1;
  EEPROM.write(3, CalStatus);
  EEPROM.write(4, highByte(CalLow));
  EEPROM.write(5, lowByte(CalLow));
  TempInt = CalLowpH * 100;
  EEPROM.write(6, highByte(TempInt));
  EEPROM.write(7, lowByte(TempInt));
 }

 if (CalCommand.startsWith("CM")) {
  CalCommand = CalCommand.substring(2);
  CalMidpH = CalCommand.toFloat();
  CalMid = GetMiddleAnalog();
  CalStatus = CalStatus | 2;
  EEPROM.write(3, CalStatus);
  EEPROM.write(8, highByte(CalMid));
  EEPROM.write(9, lowByte(CalMid));
  TempInt = CalMidpH * 100;
  EEPROM.write(10, highByte(TempInt));
  EEPROM.write(11, lowByte(TempInt));
 }

 if (CalCommand.startsWith("CU")) {
  CalCommand = CalCommand.substring(2);
  CalHighpH = CalCommand.toFloat();
  CalHigh = GetMiddleAnalog();
  CalStatus = CalStatus | 4;
  EEPROM.write(3, CalStatus);
  EEPROM.write(12, highByte(CalHigh));
  EEPROM.write(13, lowByte(CalHigh));
```

```
    TempInt = CalHighpH * 100.0;
    EEPROM.write(14, highByte(TempInt));
    EEPROM.write(15, lowByte(TempInt));
   }
   CalCommand = "";
  } // End of if (CalCommand.length() >0)
 digitalWrite(TurnOffSensorPin,LOW);
 AV = GetMiddleAnalog();
 if (AV > CalMid) {
  PHReading = CalMidpH + (CalHighpH - CalMidpH)/(CalHigh - CalMid) *(AV - CalMid);
  }
 if (AV <= CalMid) {
  PHReading = CalMidpH - (CalMidpH - CalLowpH)/(CalMid - CalLow) *(CalMid- AV);
  }
 Serial.print("pH = ");
 Serial.println(PHReading);
  if (PHReading > 2 && PHReading < 12){
  PHReading3 = PHReading2;
  PHReading2 = PHReading1;
  PHReading1= PHReading;
  if (PHReading1 > TooHigh && PHReading2 > TooHigh && PHReading3 > TooHigh) {
    digitalWrite(HighpHPin,HIGH);
   }
   else {
   digitalWrite(HighpHPin,LOW);
   }
   if (PHReading1 < TooLow && PHReading2 < TooLow && PHReading3 < TooLow) {
    digitalWrite(LowpHPin,HIGH);
   }
   else {
   digitalWrite(LowpHPin,LOW);
   }
   } // End of if PHReading > 2 && PHReading < 12
  Serial.print("pH = ");
```

```
    Serial.print(PHReading1,4);
    Serial.print(" ");
    Serial.print(PHReading2,4);
    Serial.print(" ");
    Serial.println(PHReading3,4);
    delay(1000);
  }
  else{
    digitalWrite(TurnOffSensorPin, HIGH);
  }
} // End main loop

int GetMiddleAnalog(){
  int i, j;
  int n = 5;
  int temp;
  int arr[5];
  for (i = 0; i < n; i++){
    arr[i] = analogRead(pHInputPin);
    // Important: If using circuit board from Figure 7.2, you must change above line to
    //   arr[i] = 1023 - analogRead(pHInputPin);

    delay(20);
  }
  for (i = 0; i < n; i++){
    for (j = 0; j < n-1; j++) {
      if (arr[j] > arr[j+1]) {
        int temp = arr[j];
        arr[j] = arr[j+1];
        arr[j+1] = temp;
      }
    }
  }
  return arr[2];
}// End GetMiddle
```

Sketch 7.1

This sketch is similar to previous sketches, like the moisture meter in Sketch 5.6, except that it takes action if the analog reading is either too high or too low. First, the two output relay pins are defined as 2 and 3. In addition, pin 4 is defined as TurnOffSensorPin, which can turn off power to the sensor. This is because the pH meter can go crazy if certain other sensors connected to the same Arduino are turned on in the same water, in particular the electrical conductivity (also known as a total dissolved solids meter). Because of this, I have provided for turning off the pH meter when these are turned on. I will discuss the mechanics of this later.

Next, the variables TooLow (which sets when the pH is too low) and TooHigh (which sets when it is too high) are defined as floating point variables and given a value. The values chosen for this sketch are considered minimum and maximum desirable values for fully established aquaponic systems. However, you must determine what values to set for your system, based on the particular plants and fish you have. For example, if you have a hydroponic instead of aquaponic system, you want a lower pH, around 6. The variables PHReading, PHReading1, PHReading2 and PHReading3 hold past and present pH readings. The reason for so many variables is that I have added the safety requirement that there must be three successive readings in a row outside the acceptable range before the relay is triggered. The variable AV will hold the actual raw analog reading from which pH is computed. The variable CalCommand (short for Calibration Command) is a string that will hold the calibration command you send from the serial monitor. CalLow is the raw analog input value that indicates the low benchmark pH, and CalLowpH is that pH. These are set to values of 292 and 4.0 respectively when the program starts, but will be changed once the proper calibrations are set. Likewise, CalMid, CalMidpH, CalHigh, and CalHighpH are the same for middle and high calibration. HighByte, LowByte and TempInt are temporary variables used to break up the integer values to store and retrieve them from memory. CalStatus indicates the status of the calibration. It will be 0 if none of the three reference points have been calibrated, 7 if they all have, and values in between if some of the points have been calibrated. PHEnabled is a flag that indicates whether the pH reading is enabled. As mentioned before, the pH reading must be disabled if certain other readings are taken from the same Arduino. In this chapter, PHEnabled will always be true, but I am setting it up to be controlled in later chapters.

The setup routine sets the three output pins to OUTPUT mode and sets them initially low. It also initialized serial communications so that you can see the pH readings from the serial monitor. Then it reads in stored calibrations. This is similar to when the soil moisture level to trigger watering was set and stored in Chapter 6, but a bit more complicated. The math involved in storing three pieces of information (the status of the three calibrations) in one byte involves bit manipulation, which I will not go into here. The act of storing a two-byte integer in two separate memory bytes is also complex, as we saw in chapter 5. Rather than get bogged down in high level math, I will just say that the part of the setup routine starting with
CalStatus = EEPROM.read(3);
retrieves the stored calibration from memory. I will note that storing the calibration data in memory uses the memory from byte 3 to byte 15. The soil moisture sketch used bytes 0 through 2. It is important to use different memory locations to store all the data. In anticipation of combining some of the sketches in later chapters, I am using different memory locations in each chapter.

In the loop routine, it first checks to see if PHEnabled is true. If so, the line
digitalWrite(TurnOffSensorPin, LOW);
turns off the relay that cuts power to the sensor. Cutting of this relay powers the pH sensor. (See Figure 7.1 later.)

Next, the code from the line
while (Serial.available()) {

to the line
} // //End of while loop that reads string
reads in a string from the serial monitor. That first line checks to see if there is any data coming into the serial port. The next line reads in one character, and the next adds each character to the end of the string CalCommand. This process continues until there are no more characters available from the serial port.

The lines from the line
if (CalCommand.length() >0){
to the line
} // End of if (CalCommand.length() >0)
execute the command received from the serial monitor. The first line simply checks to see if there is a command by seeing is the length of the CalCommand is more than 0. The line
CalCommand.toUpperCase();
simply converts the string to upper case in case you forgot to use upper case when you typed. It then sends the command back to the serial monitor just so you can see what you typed to check for typos.

Next, there are three if statements to see if the command string starts with either CL, CM, or CU. If any of these is true, the code within the lines contained in the if statement brackets is executed. The line
CalCommand = CalCommand.substring(2);
strips off the first to characters (e.g., CL), leaving only the number (such as 4 or 9.2). In the CL operation, the line
CalLowpH = CalCommand.toFloat();
converts the string, such as "9.2", into an actual floating point number, like 9.2. The line
CalLow = GetMiddleAnalog();
then gets the analog reading and stores it in CalLow. (I will explain the GetMiddleAnalog() function shortly.) The line
CalStatus = CalStatus | 1;
records the fact that you have performed that calibration option in CalStatus by setting the first bit of CalStatus to 1 using bit manipulation. The next three lines save CalStatus

in memory location 3 and CalMid (the analog input value) in locations 4 and 5. The next three lines store the pH value you specified in memory. The statement
TempInt = CalMidpH * 100;
converts CalMidpH, which is a floating point value, into an integer by multiplying it by 100 and rounding it off. This is done because integers are easier to save. Integers take two bytes to save and floating point variables take four. Multiplying the floating point variable by 100, converting it to an integer, and then saving it in two bytes saves two bytes of memory per variable. The next two lines store the integer value in memory locations 6 and 7. When the value is read back in the setup routine, it is divided by 100.0 to restore its original value. The value is retrieved with two decimal points of precision, which is much greater than the precision of calibration solution. Notice that the 100 is written as 100.0. It is vitally important to include the .0 in the number, because that tells the code to perform the division as floating point math. Otherwise, it would round off to an integer value, and a number stored as something like 6.8 would be retrieved as 6.

Looking at this description, you can see that it stores the current analog input value along with the value you said the pH being read has, such as 4. Thus, the Arduino now has the information of what that analog input represents. This has been a description of the operation when you input CL followed by a number. The two if statements after this perform the same operation for higher values when you input the command CM and CU.

The code after the code that performs the calibration reads analog input and stores the value in AV. Instead of reading the value here in the code, I have called a subroutine named GetMiddleAnalog(). You may recall that I mentioned in Chapter 1 that you can put sections of code in subroutines that you can jump into from multiple locations. This is an example of that. In order to filter out any possible erratic readings caused by line noise or other random events, the subroutine GetMiddleAnalog() reads the analog input five times, separated by 20 milliseconds per reading. This is done by the code

```
for (i = 0; i < n; i++){
 arr[i] = analogRead(pHInputPin);
 // Important: If using circuit board from Figure 7.2, you must change above line to
 //  arr[i] = 1023 - analogRead(pHInputPin);
 delay(20);
}
```

Note: If you are using the circuit board in Figure 7.2, be sure to heed the remarks in the code that you must use the alternate code for reading the analog pin, because that circuit outputs higher voltage for lower pH.

The sort code

```
for (i = 0; i < n; i++){
 for (j = 0; j < n-1; j++) {
  if (arr[j] > arr[j+1]) {
   int temp = arr[j];
   arr[j] = arr[j+1];
   arr[j+1] = temp;
  }
 }
}
```

then arranges these five readings in order from lowest to highest.

The line
```
return arr[2];
```
then gives the GetMiddleAnalog() subroutine name the value of the middle value, arr[2]. That is, it throws out the two highest and two lowest readings and accepts only the middle value.

Thus, the line
```
AV = GetMiddleAnalog();
```
actually sends the program to the GetMiddleAnalog() subroutine, executes that subroutine, and assigns the value computed to AV. One interesting thing to note is that the subroutine GetMiddleAnalog() does not start with the word void like the other routines we have seen so far. It starts

with int. This is because this subroutine has an integer value, unlike any routine or subroutine that starts with void and returns no value.

After AV is given the value of the middle analog reading, the next lines compute the pH from the analog input. It uses two different formulas, one if the analog reading is above the middle calibration point and one if it is below or equal to this point. What it does is estimate the value based along the slope from the measured midpoint to either the higher or lower calibration point. Fortunately, the relationship between pH and the analog reading is fairly linear within the ranges from the midpoint to the two calibration points, so this estimation is very nearly correct.

Once the pH has been computed, we get to the part of the code that acts on the pH value. First, it sends the value message to the serial port so you can read it. You could use this serial monitor display if you want to check what the actual pH readings are, and to diagnose possible problems by looking for erratic or impossible readings. In later chapters, I will give you much better ways to display information about actual values without needing to have a computer connected to the Arduino.

After sending the observed pH reading to the serial monitor, the line
if (PHReading > 2 && PHReading < 12)
checks to make sure that the pH reading is between 2 and 12. It will not execute the lines within the if statement if the reading is not within this range. The reason for this is to prevent the Arduino from acting on invalid readings. It should be impossible for the pH to actually ever be beyond this range. The normal range of an aquaponic system should be between 6.8 and 7.2, and for hydroponic systems between 5.5 and 6.2. You will certainly take action long before it gets anywhere near 4 or 10, let alone 2 or 12. However, problems like a short circuit or a loose connection can drive the apparent pH reading to 0 or 14. In fact, since the calculation of readings beyond the calibration points is an extrapolation from those points and

the output becomes increasingly nonlinear beyond them, you could get totally impossible figures like negative numbers or pH of 20 in the event of a malfunction. If you are merely connecting the Arduino to an alarm, you might want to allow the alarm to sound when you get these readings so you can check the malfunction. IF so, delete the lines

if (PHReading > 2 && PHReading < 12){

and

} // End of if PHReading > 2 && PHReading < 12

from the code. However, if you actually have the Arduino taking action based on the readings, as will be discussed shortly, you definitely want to prevent the Arduino from acting based on a malfunction.

    Once you are in the code that executes if you are getting reasonable readings, you have the lines

  PHReading3 = PHReading2;

  PHReading2 = PHReading1;

  PHReading1= PHReading;

    These store the two previous readings and the current one. Each reading is shifted back one, and PHReading1 becomes the current reading that we just took.

    We then start comparing these readings to the acceptable limits. If all three of the last three readings are higher than TooHigh, the line

digitalWrite(HighpHPin, HIGH);

turns on whatever is connected to HighpHPin. If not, the else statement turns it off. Likewise, if all three of the latest readings are below TooLow, the LowpHPin pin is turned on. If not, the else statement turns it off. The serial print statements send all three latest readings to the serial monitor so you can monitor what is going on for diagnostic purposes. The delay statement gives the probe a little chance to settle after taking a reading, and also prevents the lines on the serial monitor from scrolling by too fast to read. It also provides a little time for any unusual conditions that might affect readings, like a fish swimming past the probe, to pass. This makes sure that the three latest readings really are separate readings.

If the pH reading is not enabled (PHEnabled = false), then the else statement is executed. This turns on a relay to disconnect power to the pH circuit board. Figure 7.6 shows a circuit to do this.

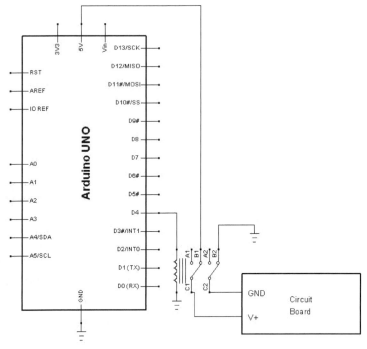

Figure 7.6

Pin 4 is connected to the DPDT relay controller pin. One relay common connector goes to the circuit board ground connection, and the other to the V+ power pin. The corresponding normally closed relay connectors go to the Arduino GND and 5V. Be sure to connect the proper pins so you do not reverse polarity on the circuit board, and to use the normally closed connections so that the power is supplied to the circuit board when the relay is OFF, not ON.

This disconnecting of the power to the pH probe is not absolutely necessary, but it does totally disconnect the pH meter from any other instruments that might cause trouble with it, and possibly damage it over time. Any sensor that actually sends current into the water, like an electrical conductivity sensor, tends to short the pH probe contacts to ground. Note that this is only necessary at all if you have one Arduino controlling several sensors. If you are using a separate Arduino to test for pH, you can skip this circuit and omit the parts of the sketch that disable the pH probe.

Now we have the question of what the output pins should be controlling. As mentioned, you could simply have them turn on an alarm by having the pins turn on a bell or light or other alarm. However, instead of simply sounding an alarm, you could have the Arduino take action automatically. You can have a tank of acid and a tank of base solution. This tank should be placed near your tank containing the fish, and preferably higher. You can then have a pump or motor controlled valve that will transfer the acid or base to the fish tank. When the pH is too high, you can have the HighpHPin pin turn on the pump or valve that adds acid to the water in your tank. When the pH is too low, the LowpHPin pin can turn on the pump or valve to add base to raise it. However, Sketch 7.1 is a bit to simplistic for that. The problem is that if you simply start pouring acid or base into the water until the pH falls back into the desired range, it will take a while for the chemicals to disperse through the water and for the pH meter to register the change in pH. You could easily add too much and overshoot the desired pH, making it too high or low the other way. The solution to this problem is to add base or acid for a short time, then pause a while for the chemical to disperse and take effect before checking to see if more is needed. Then, if the pH is still too high or low, repeat the process. Sketch 7.2 shows how to do this.

```
#include <EEPROM.h>

#define LowpHPin 2
```

```
#define HighpHPin 3
#define TurnOffSensorPin 4
#define pHInputPin A2

int OnTime = 10;
int OffTime= 120;
bool AddingAcid = false;
bool AddingBase = false;
unsigned long AddAcidStart = 0;
unsigned long AddBaseStart = 0;
unsigned long AddAcidStop = 0;
unsigned long AddBaseStop = 0;

float TooLow = 6.70;
float TooHigh = 7.10;
float PHReading;
float PHReading1;
float PHReading2;
float PHReading3;
int AV;

String CalCommand;
unsigned int CalLow = 292;
float CalLowpH = 4;
unsigned int CalMid = 497;
float CalMidpH = 6.8;
unsigned int CalHigh = 672;
float CalHighpH = 9.2;
byte HighByte;
byte LowByte;
byte CalStatus;
unsigned int TempInt;
bool PHEnabled = true;

void setup(){
  pinMode(LowpHPin, OUTPUT);
  digitalWrite(LowpHPin, LOW );
  pinMode(HighpHPin, OUTPUT);
```

```
digitalWrite(HighpHPin, LOW );
pinMode(TurnOffSensorPin, OUTPUT);
digitalWrite(TurnOffSensorPin, LOW );
Serial.begin(9600);
CalStatus = EEPROM.read(3);
if (CalStatus > 7) {
 CalStatus = 0;
 EEPROM.write(3, CalStatus);
}
Serial.println(CalStatus);
if ((CalStatus & 1) == 1){
 HighByte = EEPROM.read(4);
 LowByte =  EEPROM.read(5);
 if (HighByte + LowByte < 510) {
  CalLow = (HighByte << 8) + LowByte;
 }
 HighByte = EEPROM.read(6);
 LowByte =  EEPROM.read(7);
 if (HighByte + LowByte < 510) {
   TempInt = (HighByte << 8) + LowByte;
   CalLowpH = TempInt / 100.0;
 }
}
Serial.print("Low pH: ");
Serial.print(CalLow);
Serial.print("   ");
Serial.println(CalLowpH);

if ((CalStatus & 2) == 2){
 HighByte = EEPROM.read(8);
 LowByte =  EEPROM.read(9);
 if (HighByte + LowByte < 510) {
   CalMid = (HighByte << 8) + LowByte;
 }
 HighByte = EEPROM.read(10);
 LowByte =  EEPROM.read(11);
 if (HighByte + LowByte < 510) {
   TempInt = (HighByte << 8) + LowByte;
```

```
      CalMidpH = TempInt / 100.0;
    }
  }
  Serial.print("Mid pH: ");
  Serial.print(CalMid);
  Serial.print("   ");
  Serial.println(CalMidpH);
  if ((CalStatus & 4) == 4){
    HighByte = EEPROM.read(12);
    LowByte =  EEPROM.read(13);
    if (HighByte + LowByte < 510) {
      CalHigh = (HighByte << 8) + LowByte;
    }
    Serial.println(CalHigh);
    HighByte = EEPROM.read(14);
    LowByte =  EEPROM.read(15);
    if (HighByte + LowByte < 510) {
      TempInt = (HighByte << 8) + LowByte;
      CalHighpH = TempInt / 100.0;
    }
  }
  Serial.print("High pH: ");
  Serial.print(CalHigh);
  Serial.print("   ");
  Serial.println(CalHighpH);
}// End setup

void loop() {
  if (PHEnabled) {
    digitalWrite(TurnOffSensorPin, LOW);
    while (Serial.available()) {
      delay(4);  //delay to allow buffer to fill
      if (Serial.available() >0) {
        char c = Serial.read();   //gets one byte from serial buffer
        CalCommand += c; //makes the string readString
      }
    } //End of while loop that reads string
```

```
if (CalCommand.length() >0 ){
 CalCommand.toUpperCase();
 Serial.println(CalCommand);
 if (CalCommand.startsWith("CL")) {
  CalCommand = CalCommand.substring(2);
  CalLowpH = CalCommand.toFloat();
  CalLow = GetMiddleAnalog();
  CalStatus = CalStatus | 1;
  EEPROM.write(3, CalStatus);
  EEPROM.write(4, highByte(CalLow));
  EEPROM.write(5, lowByte(CalLow));
  TempInt = CalLowpH * 100;
  EEPROM.write(6, highByte(TempInt));
  EEPROM.write(7, lowByte(TempInt));
 }
 if (CalCommand.startsWith("CM")) {
  CalCommand = CalCommand.substring(2);
  CalMidpH = CalCommand.toFloat();
  CalMid = GetMiddleAnalog();
  CalStatus = CalStatus | 2;
  EEPROM.write(3, CalStatus);
  EEPROM.write(8, highByte(CalMid));
  EEPROM.write(9, lowByte(CalMid));
  TempInt = CalMidpH * 100;
  EEPROM.write(10, highByte(TempInt));
  EEPROM.write(11, lowByte(TempInt));
 }
 if (CalCommand.startsWith("CU")) {
  CalCommand = CalCommand.substring(2);
  CalHighpH = CalCommand.toFloat();
  CalHigh = GetMiddleAnalog();
  CalStatus = CalStatus | 4;
  EEPROM.write(3, CalStatus);
  EEPROM.write(12, highByte(CalHigh));
  EEPROM.write(13, lowByte(CalHigh));
  TempInt = CalHighpH * 100.0;
  EEPROM.write(14, highByte(TempInt));
  EEPROM.write(15, lowByte(TempInt));
```

```
    }
    CalCommand = "";
  } // End of if (CalCommand.length() >0 )

  AV = GetMiddleAnalog();;
  if (AV > CalMid) {
    PHReading  =  CalMidpH  +  (CalHighpH - CalMidpH)/(CalHigh - CalMid) *(AV - CalMid);
  }
  if (AV <= CalMid) {
    PHReading  =  CalMidpH  -  (CalMidpH - CalLowpH)/(CalMid - CalLow ) *(CalMid- AV);
  }
  Serial.print("pH = ");
  Serial.println(PHReading);
  if (PHReading > 2 && PHReading < 12){
    PHReading3 = PHReading2;
    PHReading2 = PHReading1;
    PHReading1= PHReading;
    if (PHReading1 > TooHigh && PHReading2 > TooHigh && PHReading3 > TooHigh) {
      if (!AddingAcid) {
        if ((millis() - AddAcidStop)/1000 > OffTime || AddAcidStop > millis()) {
          digitalWrite(HighpHPin,HIGH);
          AddingAcid = true;
          AddAcidStart = millis();
        }
      }
    } // End of test for pH being too high last three readings
    if (AddingAcid) {
      if ((millis() - AddAcidStart)/1000 > OnTime || AddAcidStart > millis()) {
        digitalWrite(HighpHPin,LOW);
        AddingAcid = false;
        AddAcidStop = millis();
      }
    }
```

```
   if (PHReading1 < TooLow && PHReading2 < TooLow
&& PHReading3 < TooLow) {
     if (!AddingBase) {
      if ((millis() - AddBaseStop)/1000 > OffTime ||
AddBaseStop > millis()) {
        digitalWrite(LowpHPin,HIGH);
        AddingBase = true;
        AddBaseStart = millis();
       }
     }
   } // End if readings too low
   if (AddingBase) {
     if ((millis() - AddBaseStart)/1000> OnTime ||
AddBaseStart > millis()) {
      digitalWrite(LowpHPin,LOW);
      AddingBase = false;
      AddBaseStop = millis();
     }
   }
   } // End of if PHReading > 2 && PHReading < 12

  Serial.print("pH = ");
  Serial.print(PHReading1,4);
  Serial.print("   ");
  Serial.print(PHReading2,4);
  Serial.print("   ");
  Serial.println(PHReading3,4);
  delay(1000);
  } // End ph enabled test
  else{
    digitalWrite(TurnOffSensorPin, HIGH);
  }
} // End main loop

int GetMiddleAnalog(){
  int i, j;
  int n = 5;
  int temp;
```

```
  int arr[5];
  for (i = 0; i < n; i++){
    arr[i] = analogRead(pHInputPin);
    // Important: If using circuit board from Figure 7.2, you must change above line to
    //  arr[i] = 1023 - analogRead(pHInputPin);
    delay(20);
  }
  for (i = 0; i < n; i++){
    for (j = 0; j < n-1; j++) {
      if (arr[j] > arr[j+1]) {
        int temp = arr[j];
        arr[j] = arr[j+1];
        arr[j+1] = temp;
      }
    }
  }
  return arr[2];
}// End GetMiddleAnalog
```

Sketch 7.2

This sketch is based on Sketch 7.1, so I will discuss only the differences between them. In this sketch, I have added OnTime, the time the pump or valve is adding the acid or base to the water to adjust the pH, and OffTime, the pause time between doses of this chemical while the system is waiting for it is assimilated. These are expressed in seconds. In this example, I set an OnTime of 10 seconds and an OffTime of 120 seconds. The actual values you will need to use will depend of a variety of factors, such as the total volume of the water in your system, the rate of flow of the chemical through the pump or valve, and the concentration of the chemical being added. On the subject of concentration, I recommend diluting the acid and base solutions if they are in a concentrated form, to allow the amount added to be more carefully controlled.

We have flag variables AddingAcid and AddingBase to keep track of whether acid or base are being added (pump or valve on). The variables AddAcidStart, AddBaseStart, AddAcidStop, and AddBaseStop record the times when acid or base starts and stops being added.

The next change is after the line
if (PHReading1 > TooHigh && PHReading2 > TooHigh && PHReading3 > TooHigh)
checks to see if all three of the latest readings are too high. Instead of simply turning on a pin immediately, the next line checks to see if you are currently not adding acid. If you are not adding acid, the line
if (millis() - AddAcidStop > OffTime * 1000 || AddAcidStop > millis())
checks to see if the current time minus the time you stopped adding acid is greater than the pause time, or if the millis() function has rolled over. If either of these is true, the code goes on to the lines
digitalWrite(HighpHPin, HIGH);
AddingAcid = true;
AddAcidStart = millis();
These lines first turn on the acid flow by setting the HighpHPin pin HIGH. Then the second line sets the flag AddingAcid to true to keep track of the fact that acid is being added. The third line records the time when acid started being added. Since these lines will not be executed unless AddingAcid is false, they will not be executed again until the acid has been turned off. In fact, they will not be executed again until the acid has been stopped and the time limit OffTime has passed.

After this, we come to a set of lines that will only be executed if AddingAcid is true because of the line if (AddingAcid). If this is true, the code then checks the condition
if (millis() - AddAcidStart > OnTime * 1000 || AddAcidStart > millis())

This checks to see if the time since the acid was started is greater than OnTime, or the millis() function has rolled over. If so, the lines
digitalWrite(HighpHPin, LOW);
AddingAcid = false;
AddAcidStop = millis();
turn off the acid flow by setting HighpHPin pin low, mark AddingAcid as false to indicate that the acid is no longer being added, and record the time when the acid flow stopped.

Thus, we have a flip flopping between the acid being turned on and off. Each time it is turned on, the time is recorded so the code will know when to turn it off. Each time it is turned off, the time is recorded so the code will know when to turn it back on. However, the acid will only be turned back on if the pH is still too high. Thus, once the pH has been lowered enough, the acid is not switched on after being turned off. The same process is duplicated for adding base when the pH is too low.

So far we have a sketch that turn on an alarm if the pH is too high or low and a sketch that actually acts on its own in those cases. We can combine the best features of the two. We can have a sketch that turns on an alarm if the pH gets below a certain level, and then takes action if it gets further below that level. Likewise, it can turn on an alarm if the pH gets above a certain level, and take action if it gets even further above that level. This is the best of both worlds, because it allows you to exercise your human judgment about what to do first, but then does correct the situation if you are unable to (such as if you are away from the garden). Sketch 7.3 does this by combining Sketch 7.1 and 7.2.

```
#include <EEPROM.h>
#define LowpHPin 2
#define HighpHPin 3
#define TurnOffSensorPin 4
#define LowpHAlarmPin 5
```

```
#define HighpHAlarmPin 6
#define pHInputPin A2

int OnTime = 10;
int OffTime= 120;
bool AddingAcid = false;
bool AddingBase = false;
unsigned long AddAcidStart = 0;
unsigned long AddBaseStart = 0;
unsigned long AddAcidStop = 0;
unsigned long AddBaseStop = 0;

float TooLow = 6.60;
float TooHigh = 7.20;
float LowAlarm = 6.8;
float HighAlarm = 7.0;
float PHReading;
float PHReading1;
float PHReading2;
float PHReading3;
int AV;

String CalCommand;
unsigned int CalLow = 292;
float CalLowpH = 4;
unsigned int CalMid = 497;
float CalMidpH = 6.8;
unsigned int CalHigh = 672;
float CalHighpH = 9.2;
byte HighByte;
byte LowByte;
byte CalStatus;
unsigned int TempInt;
bool PHEnabled = true;

void setup(){
  pinMode(LowpHPin, OUTPUT);
  digitalWrite(LowpHPin, LOW);
```

```
pinMode(HighpHPin, OUTPUT);
digitalWrite(HighpHPin, LOW);
pinMode(LowpHAlarmPin, OUTPUT);
digitalWrite(LowpHAlarmPin, LOW);
pinMode(HighpHAlarmPin, OUTPUT);
digitalWrite(HighpHAlarmPin, LOW);
pinMode(TurnOffSensorPin, OUTPUT);
digitalWrite(TurnOffSensorPin, LOW);
Serial.begin(9600);
CalStatus = EEPROM.read(3);
if (CalStatus > 7) {
 CalStatus = 0;
 EEPROM.write(3, CalStatus);
}
Serial.println(CalStatus);
if ((CalStatus & 1) == 1){
  HighByte = EEPROM.read(4);
  LowByte = EEPROM.read(5);
  if (HighByte + LowByte < 510) {
   CalLow = (HighByte << 8) + LowByte;
  }
 HighByte = EEPROM.read(6);
 LowByte = EEPROM.read(7);
 if (HighByte + LowByte < 510) {
    TempInt = (HighByte << 8) + LowByte;
    CalLowpH = TempInt / 100.0;
 }
}
Serial.print("Low pH: ");
Serial.print(CalLow);
Serial.print("   ");
Serial.println(CalLowpH);

if ((CalStatus & 2) == 2){
 HighByte = EEPROM.read(8);
  LowByte = EEPROM.read(9);
  if (HighByte + LowByte < 510) {
    CalMid = (HighByte << 8) + LowByte;
```

```
    }
    HighByte = EEPROM.read(10);
    LowByte = EEPROM.read(11);
    if (HighByte + LowByte < 510) {
      TempInt = (HighByte << 8) + LowByte;
      CalMidpH = TempInt / 100.0;
    }
  }
  Serial.print("Mid pH: ");
  Serial.print(CalMid);
  Serial.print("   ");
  Serial.println(CalMidpH);
  if ((CalStatus & 4) == 4){
    HighByte = EEPROM.read(12);
    LowByte = EEPROM.read(13);
    if (HighByte + LowByte < 510) {
      CalHigh = (HighByte << 8) + LowByte;
    }
    Serial.println(CalHigh);
    HighByte = EEPROM.read(14);
    LowByte = EEPROM.read(15);
    if (HighByte + LowByte < 510) {
      TempInt = (HighByte << 8) + LowByte;
      CalHighpH = TempInt / 100.0;
    }
  }
  Serial.print("High pH: ");
  Serial.print(CalHigh);
  Serial.print("   ");
  Serial.println(CalHighpH);
}// End setup

void loop() {
  if (PHEnabled) {
    digitalWrite(TurnOffSensorPin, LOW);
    while (Serial.available()) {
      delay(4); //delay to allow buffer to fill
      if (Serial.available() >0) {
```

```
    char c = Serial.read();
    CalCommand += c;
  }
} //End of while loop that reads string
if (CalCommand.length() >0){
  CalCommand.toUpperCase();
  Serial.println(CalCommand);
  if (CalCommand.startsWith("CL")) {
    CalCommand = CalCommand.substring(2);
    CalLowpH = CalCommand.toFloat();
    CalLow = GetMiddleAnalog();
    CalStatus = CalStatus | 1;
    EEPROM.write(3, CalStatus);
    EEPROM.write(4, highByte(CalLow));
    EEPROM.write(5, lowByte(CalLow));
    TempInt = CalLowpH * 100;
    EEPROM.write(6, highByte(TempInt));
    EEPROM.write(7, lowByte(TempInt));
  }
  if (CalCommand.startsWith("CM")) {
    CalCommand = CalCommand.substring(2);
    CalMidpH = CalCommand.toFloat();
    CalMid = GetMiddleAnalog();
    CalStatus = CalStatus | 2;
    EEPROM.write(3, CalStatus);
    EEPROM.write(8, highByte(CalMid));
    EEPROM.write(9, lowByte(CalMid));
    TempInt = CalMidpH * 100;
    EEPROM.write(10, highByte(TempInt));
    EEPROM.write(11, lowByte(TempInt));
  }
  if (CalCommand.startsWith("CU")) {
    CalCommand = CalCommand.substring(2);
    CalHighpH = CalCommand.toFloat();
    CalHigh = GetMiddleAnalog();
    CalStatus = CalStatus | 4;
    EEPROM.write(3, CalStatus);
    EEPROM.write(12, highByte(CalHigh));
```

```
    EEPROM.write(13, lowByte(CalHigh));
    TempInt = CalHighpH * 100.0;
    EEPROM.write(14, highByte(TempInt));
    EEPROM.write(15, lowByte(TempInt));
   }
   CalCommand = "";
 } // End of if (CalCommand.length() >0)

 AV = GetMiddleAnalog();
 if (AV > CalMid) {
   PHReading  =  CalMidpH  +  (CalHighpH  -
CalMidpH)/(CalHigh - CalMid) *(AV - CalMid);
   }
 if (AV <= CalMid) {
   PHReading  =  CalMidpH  -  (CalMidpH  -
CalLowpH)/(CalMid - CalLow) *(CalMid- AV);
   }
 Serial.print("pH = ");
 Serial.println(PHReading);
  if (PHReading1 > HighAlarm && PHReading2 >
HighAlarm && PHReading3 > HighAlarm) {
    digitalWrite(HighpHAlarmPin,HIGH);
   }
   else {
    digitalWrite(HighpHAlarmPin,LOW);
   }
   if (PHReading1 < LowAlarm && PHReading2 <
LowAlarm && PHReading3 < LowAlarm) {
    digitalWrite(LowpHAlarmPin,HIGH);
   }
   else {
    digitalWrite(LowpHAlarmPin,LOW);
   }
  if (PHReading > 2 && PHReading < 12){
    PHReading3 = PHReading2;
    PHReading2 = PHReading1;
    PHReading1= PHReading;
```

```
    if (PHReading1 > TooHigh && PHReading2 > TooHigh
&& PHReading3 > TooHigh) {
      if (!AddingAcid) {
        if ((millis() - AddAcidStop)/1000 > OffTime ||
AddAcidStop > millis()) {
          digitalWrite(HighpHPin,HIGH);
          AddingAcid = true;
          AddAcidStart = millis();
        }
      }
    } // End of test for pH being too high last three readings
    if (AddingAcid) {
      if ((millis() - AddAcidStart)/1000 > OnTime ||
AddAcidStart > millis()) {
        digitalWrite(HighpHPin,LOW);
        AddingAcid = false;
        AddAcidStop = millis();
      }
    }

    if (PHReading1 < TooLow && PHReading2 < TooLow
&& PHReading3 < TooLow) {
      if (!AddingBase) {
        if ((millis() - AddBaseStop)/1000 > OffTime ||
AddBaseStop > millis()) {
          digitalWrite(LowpHPin,HIGH);
          AddingBase = true;
          AddBaseStart = millis();
        }
      }
    } // End if readings too low
    if (AddingBase) {
      if ((millis() - AddBaseStart)/1000> OnTime ||
AddBaseStart > millis()) {
        digitalWrite(LowpHPin,LOW);
        AddingBase = false;
        AddBaseStop = millis();
      }
```

```
    }
} // End of if PHReading > 2 && PHReading < 12

  Serial.print("pH = ");
  Serial.print(PHReading1,4);
  Serial.print("  ");
  Serial.print(PHReading2,4);
  Serial.print("  ");
  Serial.println(PHReading3,4);
  delay(1000);
  } // End ph enabled test
  else{
    digitalWrite(TurnOffSensorPin, HIGH);
  }
} //  End main loop

int GetMiddleAnalog(){
  int i, j;
  int n = 5;
  int temp;
  int arr[5];
  for (i = 0; i < n; i++){
    arr[i] = analogRead(pHInputPin);
    // Important: If using circuit board from Figure 7.2, you must change above line to
    //  arr[i] = 1023 - analogRead(pHInputPin);
    delay(20);
  }
  for (i = 0; i < n; i++){
    for (j = 0; j < n-1; j++) {
      if (arr[j] > arr[j+1]) {
        int temp = arr[j];
        arr[j] = arr[j+1];
        arr[j+1] = temp;
      }
    }
  }
  return arr[2];
```

}// End GetMiddleAnalog

Sketch 7.3

Here I have simply added a few lines to Sketch 7.2. I have defined LowpHAlarmPin as 5 and HighpHAlarmPin as 6. You will therefore connect whatever device you use to signal low and high pH to these pins. I have set the pH level to trigger a low alarm (LowAlarm) to 6.8 and the high pH alarm level (HighAlarm) to 7.0. I have also lowered the level at which direct action is taken for low pH (TooLow) and raised the level at which direct action is taken for high pH (TooHigh). You obviously want the alarm signal to happen before the Arduino takes action itself, to give you time to do something directly so the Arduino will not have to. In the main loop, I have added the lines

```
  if (PHReading1 > HighAlarm && PHReading2 > HighAlarm && PHReading3 > HighAlarm) {
    digitalWrite(HighpHAlarmPin, HIGH);
  }
  else {
    digitalWrite(HighpHAlarmPin, LOW);
  }
  if (PHReading1 < LowAlarm && PHReading2 < LowAlarm && PHReading3 < LowAlarm) {
    digitalWrite(LowpHAlarmPin, HIGH);
  }
  else {
    digitalWrite(LowpHAlarmPin, LOW);
  }
```

These are taken straight out of Sketch 7.1, with a few of the variable names changed so as not to conflict with the variables used in Sketch 7.2.

Note that I put these outside of the
if (PHReading > 2 && PHReading < 12)

condition. This means that the alarm will signal even if the low or high readings are due to a malfunction. This can be handy, because if the pH meter does malfunction (short out or lose connection) and start giving continuous readings below 2 or above 12, it would no longer be monitoring your system at all. An additional possible problem is that when the probe starts to deteriorate, as it eventually will after a year or two, the readings can drift a bit. They will not be completely ridiculous, but they could be off by a significant fraction of a pH. Considering these two possibilities, the wise action to take is to manually test the pH if the alarm signals. If the manual test tells you that the pH really is off, you can adjust the pH manually. If the pH is not outside the alarm limits, connect the Arduino to a computer to get the pH readings it is getting. (As mentioned, I will give you better methods to read the Arduino directly in later chapters.) If the readings are totally ridiculous, you have a severe problem like a loose connection that you need to fix. If the readings are just a bit off, you can recalibrate the probe as described earlier in this chapter. A quick recalibration technique would be to record the pH reading you are getting from the manual test (assuming you have confidence that it is correct) and send the Arduino the command CM followed by this pH reading. This will adjust the center reading to the reading you got manually. A more thorough recalibration would be to take the probe out of your water tank and recalibrate using all three standardized solutions.

Chapter 8

Electrical conductivity (total dissolved solids)

You sometimes want to track the total dissolved solids (TDS) in your water. Too low a level can mean that there are not enough nutrients in the water for your plants. Too high can indicate a serious problem, like your bacterial are not converting ammonia and nitrites to nitrates, or your plants are not absorbing nitrates, or you have a dead rotting fish in your tank. One interesting test you can conduct is to measure the TDS in the water in your fish tank and also just as it exits your plant area, to see how much difference there is. This may be able to monitor how well your bacteria and plants are absorbing ammonia and nitrites.

Monitoring TDS can be done with an electronic probe, similar to the pH probe or the temperature probe discussed in previous chapters. These probes measure the electrical conductivity (EC) of the water, and are therefore usually called EC probes rather than TDS probes. The more TDS you have in the water, the higher the conductivity of the water, since dissolved solids help conduct electricity.

There are two ways to obtain probes. You can buy one, or make your own. Most EC probes are very expensive (hundreds of dollars) and are not really compatible with Arduinos. However, I have found one company, EC/pH Transmitters, that sells a probe and circuit board specifically designed for Arduinos at a fairly reasonable price of $69.00 US plus shipping (about $6.00). The Web site address to order this device is
http://webpages.charter.net/tdsmeter/products.html
This page has multiple products. You will be looking for the one labeled Model A1003v1 Arduino EC Sensor. This comes in three models with different ranges: 0 to 50, 0 to 500, and 0 to 5000. These are in microsiemens, a measure of conductivity. I recommend the 0 to 500 model for

aquaponic systems. This will measure up to about 282 PPM, which is probably higher than you would want in an aquaponic system. If you have a hydroponic system instead, I recommend the 0 to 5000 range unit, which can measure up to 2820 PPM. Figure 8.1 is a picture of this device.

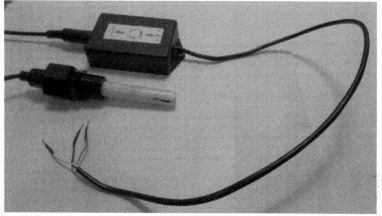

Figure 8.1

The probe plugs into the box, and the box has three wires coming from it. The red wire goes to the Arduino 5V, the blue wire goes to the Arduino GND, and the white wire connects to any Arduino analog input.

The output to the Arduino is linear to the EC of the liquid. Once calibrated, it outputs 1 volt for every 100 microsiemens (or 1000 microsiemens if you get the 0 to 5000 unit). I should mention, however, that although it is advertised as going up to 500 microsiemens, which would be a maximum output of 5 volts, it actually has a maximum range of 440 microsiemens (4.4 volts). This is because the power supply from the Arduino is 5 volts, and there is about a .6 volts loss within the circuitry. It can get a bit higher (like 4.8 volts) if you power the probe with a separate power supply like 6 or 9 volts, but this hardly seems worth it to get such a tiny increase in range.

You will need to calibrate the sensor. There is a small screw on the box that calibrates the circuit. See Figure 8.2.

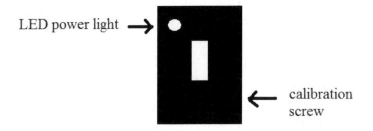

Figure 8.2

To calibrate the sensor, you need to put the sensor into a solution with a known EC or TDS, have the Arduino display the reading, and then turn the screw until the output from the Arduino matches the EC or TDS of the solution. To obtain a solution of known EC or TDS, you can buy a calibration solution designed for that purpose, or you can use your own solution and test it with a commercial EC or TDS meter. I generally find the latter better. The main reason is that it is best to calibrate the meter at an EC or TDS level that is the same as the most desirable level for your aquaponic or hydroponic system. That is, simply make sure your system is at the desirable level, test the EC or TDS levels by other means, and then put the probe into the water and calibrate the probe.

To determine the EC or TDS of your water, you can use a commercial EC or TDS meter, like the one shown in Figure 8.3.

Figure 8.3

You can buy these on Amazon.com for about $10 if you do not already have one, or get a better quality one for a bit more. One advantage of the better quality ones is that some of them compensate for temperature, which can affect EC readings (discussed later). Once you know the levels of TDS in your water, run an Arduino sketch to get repeated readings of the EC and TDS of your water from the Arduino. While looking at these readings, just adjust the screw on the probe box until the reading matches the previously measured concentration of your water. Sketch 8.1 below sends repeated EC and TDS readings to the serial port.

```
const int Probe = 500;
const int Convert = 250; // or 320 or 350
int A0V;
unsigned int EC;
unsigned int PPM;

void setup(){
  Serial.begin(9600);
}// End setup

void loop() {
  A0V = analogRead(A0);
  EC = map(A0V, 0, 1023, 0, Probe);
  PPM = map(A0V, 0, 1023, 0, Convert);
  Serial.print("A0 = ");
  Serial.print(A0V);
  Serial.print(" = ");
  Serial.print((A0V/1023.0)*5);
  Serial.println(" V");
  Serial.print("EC = ");
  Serial.println(EC);
  Serial.print("TDS = ");
  Serial.print(PPM);
  Serial.println(" PPM");
  Serial.println();
  delay(5000);
} // End main loop
```

Sketch 8.1

In this sketch, Probe is the upper range of your probe. I have set it to 500 in this sketch. If you are using the 0 to 50 or 0 to 5000 range probe, change Probe to match your value. A0V is the number taken from the analog input pin, EC is the EC converted from that number, and PPM is the parts per million TDS. A0V is read from the analog pin A0, which has a value from 0 to 1023. The map functions convert this value to EC and PPM. The Serial.print statements then send the calculations to the serial monitor, in a form like

A0 = 337 = 1.65 V
EC = 164
TDS = 82 PPM

This gives the raw A0 reading (336 in this case), what it equals in actual volts input, the calculated EC in microsiemens, and the associated TDS in PPM. Reading these, you can turn the screw on the box until the output on the serial monitor matches the EC or TDS of your solution. I have it outputting in both EC and TDS because you may have a meter or other method of measuring your test solution that uses either.

At this point, I should mention that there are several calculations to convert EC to TDS that give different results. For 1000 microsiemens, some give 500 PPM, some give 640 PPM, and some give 700 PPM. The reason is that different dissolved solids in the water have different conductivity. Thus, 1000 PPM of sodium sulfate will cause a different EC than 1000 PPM of sodium bicarbonate or sodium chloride or some other compound. In reality, any solution is almost certain to actually contain a mixture of several compounds. Thus, the conversion factor is actually fairly arbitrary. I have used the 500 value because some experts claim that this is the one that most closely matches the compounds in a hydroponic solution. However, you can see that I have set up the sketch so that this value is made at the beginning with the statement

const int Convert =250;

so you can easily change this if you prefer one of the other conversion factors. Make Convert equal to 0.5 times the value (500, 640, 700, etc.) you want 1000 microsiemens to be in PPM.

Now that you have the probe calibrated, let's do something useful with it. This requires a sketch very similar to some of the ones we have used in previous chapters that will activate a relay if the levels get too high or low. Sketch 8.2 is an example.

```
#define LowECPin 5
#define HighECPin 6
#define TurnOnSensorPin 7

const int Probe = 500;
int Convert = 250; // or 320 or 350
unsigned int MaxEC = 20;
unsigned int MinEC = 2;
unsigned int MaxTDS = 10;
unsigned int MinTDS = 1;
unsigned long ECMeasureDelay = 600;
unsigned long PreviousTime = 0;
int A0V;
unsigned int EC;
unsigned int PPM;

void setup(){
  Serial.begin(9600);
  pinMode(LowECPin, OUTPUT);
  digitalWrite(LowECPin, LOW);
  pinMode(HighECPin, OUTPUT);
  digitalWrite(HighECPin, LOW);
  pinMode(TurnOnSensorPin, OUTPUT);
  digitalWrite(TurnOnSensorPin, LOW);
  Serial.print("Delay = ");
  Serial.println(ECMeasureDelay * 1000);
}// End setup
```

```
void loop() {
  if (millis() < PreviousTime) {PreviousTime = 0;}
  if (millis() - PreviousTime >= ECMeasureDelay * 1000) {
  Serial.print("Time = ");
  Serial.println(millis() - PreviousTime);
  A0V = GetMiddleAnalog();
  EC = map(A0V, 0, 1023, 0, Probe);
  PPM = map(A0V, 0, 1023, 0, Convert);
  Serial.print("EC = ");
  Serial.println(EC);
  Serial.print("PPM = ");
  Serial.println(PPM);
  Serial.println();
  if (PPM > MaxTDS) {
    digitalWrite(HighECPin,HIGH);
  }
  else {
    digitalWrite(HighECPin,LOW);
  }
  if (PPM < MinTDS) {
    digitalWrite(LowECPin,HIGH);
  }
  else {
    digitalWrite(LowECPin,LOW);
  }
  PreviousTime = millis();
  }
} // End main loop

int GetMiddleAnalog(){
  int i, j;
  int n = 5;
  int temp;
  int arr[5];
  digitalWrite(TurnOnSensorPin, HIGH);
  delay(500);
  for (i = 0; i < n; i++){
    arr[i] = analogRead(A0);
```

```
  delay(200);
}
digitalWrite(TurnOnSensorPin, LOW);
for (i = 0; i < n; i++){
  for (j = 0; j < n-1; j++) {
    if (arr[j] > arr[j+1]) {
      int temp = arr[j];
      arr[j] = arr[j+1];
      arr[j+1] = temp;
    }
  }
}
  return arr[2];
}// End GetMiddle
```
Sketch 8.2

First, we define the output pins that will be used to turn on relays when the EC gets too high or low, LowECPin and HighECPin. We also define the pin that turns on and off power to the sensor. Because the EC sensor runs power directly to the water, it can short out other sensors, especially pH probes, in the water. If you want to run a pH probe, and possibly some other sensors, from the same Arduino, you need to be able to completely shut off power to the EC meter. The circuit for this is shown in Figure 8.3.

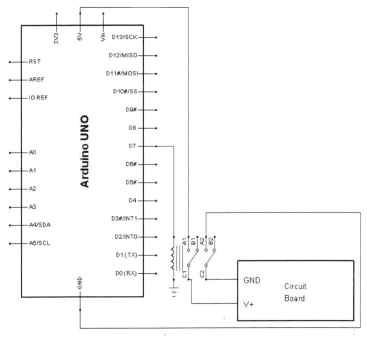

Figure 8.3

When the power pin (D7 in the sketch and diagram, but you can change that if you want) goes HIGH, the relay closes and power is supplied to the EC meter. When the power pin goes LOW, is totally cut off to the EC sensor. If you have no other sensors connected to the Arduino that could be shorted out by either a ground or V+ connection being in the water, you can omit the relay and connect the sensor directly. However, cutting power entirely to the EC meter does conserve power and prolong the life of the meter, so having the relay in this circuit is not a bad idea anyway.

As in Sketch 8.1, Convert is the conversion factor to convert your EC reading to TDS PPM. MaxEC is the value of EC that you want to trigger the relay to respond to too high EC. MinEC is the level of EC that you want to trigger the relay to respond to too low and EC. MaxTDS is the PPM TDS you want to trigger the relay for too high TDS. MinTDS is the level at which you want to trigger the relay for too low TDS. You can set these to any level you want. The reason I am providing both of these in the sketch is that some people prefer to measure the TDS as EC and some people prefer to measure them as PPM. You can use whichever you want in your sketch, and ignore the other.

The variable ECMeasureDelay is how many seconds to go between taking an EC measurement, in seconds. I have selected 600, which is ten minutes, but you can set whatever you like. The other variables defined at the beginning of this sketch are used internally and you do not need to select.

The setup routine initializes the output pins described previously. I have included initializing the serial port in case you want to add some diagnostic serial print statements.

This sketch uses a GetMiddleAnalog subroutine like previous sketches to get the middle analog readings, in order to reject any brief spikes due to line noise or other problems. This is basically the standard GetMiddleAnalog subroutine, except that it includes the lines
digitalWrite (TurnOnSensorPin, HIGH);
delay(500);
to turn on the relay to power the sensor and then delay 500 milliseconds (one half second) to allow power to the unit to come on completely. It also has the line
digitalWrite(TurnOnSensorPin, LOW);
to turn off the power when it is finished getting the readings.

The main loop has the usual code to see if the time since the last measurement is more than or equal to ECMeasureDelay seconds. If so, it gets the middle analog reading and stores in A0V. The statements
EC = map(A0V, 0, 1023, 0, 500);
PPM = map(A0V, 0, 1023, 0, Convert);
map the raw analog input values in A0V, which can range from 0 to 1023, to an EC range of 0 to 500 and a TDS PPM range of 0 to the value of Convert. The
if (PPM > MaxTDS) {

statement checks to see if the PPM value is greater than the maximum acceptable value you have set. If so, the
digitalWrite(HighECPin,HIGH);
statement turns on the relay to turn on a filter pump, alarm, or whatever you want it to turn on. If PPM is not greater than MaxTDS, the else statement turns off the relay. Of course, if the relay has not already been turned on, this has no effect. Likewise, if PPM is less than MinTDS, the
if (PPM < MinTDS) {
statement turns on the other relay, and the following else statement turns it off when PPM rises above MinTDS.

Since the program also computes EC and there is a MaxEC and MinEC set, you can replace PPM with EC and MaxTDS with MaxEC and MinTDS with MinEC in these if statements to have the code base its decisions on EC instead of TDS. It is more common to have the instructions for your aquaponic or hydroponic garden express desirable levels in PPM TDS, but if your instructions refer to EC levels, you have this option.

After running the tests for too high or low TDS, the
PreviousTime = millis();
statement records the time of this reading to allow the timer to delay the next test until millis() - PreviousTime is greater than the set time between readings.

I mentioned that the probe comes in three ranges: 0 to 50, 0 to 500, and 0 to 5000. The advantage of a higher range is, obviously, that it can measure greater amounts without going off the scale. The disadvantage is that you get poorer resolution in the lower readings. For example, if your expected readings might go from 25 to 75, the 0 to 50 range probe will not be able to read the higher ranges at all. However, the 0 to 500 probe will not be very precise measuring the difference in EC between 25 and 30. You can adjust the precision somewhat under software control using the analogReference() command. This command changes the range of the analog input pins. As explained previously, the normal range for the analog pins is 0 to 5 volts. If your EC varies from 25 to 75 and you are using the

0 to 500 probe, the output is only 0.25 to .75 volts. This does not show up as a big change on a 5 volt range. Since the readings of the analog input go from 0 to 1023, this gives readings from 51 to 153. Using the analogReference(INTERNAL) command on the Arduino Uno or analogReference(INTERNAL1V1) on the Mega, you can change the range of the analog pin from 5 volts to 1.1 volts. At that range, the 0.25 to 0.75 volts would read as 232 to 697. This converts the range on the 0 to 500 probe to 0 to 110, with better resolution for these values. On the Mega, you also have analogReference(INTERNAL2V56), which changes the upper voltage range to 2.56 volts. This converts the 0 to 500 probe to 0 to 256. You can not only set the range you want, you can have the sketch automatically select which range to use. Sketch 8.3 does this.

```
#define LowECPin 5
#define HighECPin 6
#define TurnOnSensorPin 7
const float MaxAnalog = 1023;
const int Probe = 500;
int Convert = 250; // or 320 or 350
unsigned int MaxEC = 20;
unsigned int MinEC = 2;
unsigned int MaxTDS = 10;
unsigned int MinTDS = 1;
unsigned long ECMeasureDelay = 600;
unsigned long PreviousTime = 0;
int A0V;
unsigned int EC;
unsigned int PPM;
bool Lower = false;

void setup(){
  Serial.begin(9600);
  pinMode(LowECPin, OUTPUT);
  digitalWrite(LowECPin, LOW);
```

```
  pinMode(HighECPin, OUTPUT);
  digitalWrite(HighECPin, LOW);
  pinMode(TurnOnSensorPin, OUTPUT);
  digitalWrite(TurnOnSensorPin, LOW);
  Serial.print("Delay = ");
  Serial.println(ECMeasureDelay * 1000);
}// End setup

void loop() {
  if (millis() < PreviousTime) {PreviousTime = 0;}
  if (millis() - PreviousTime >= ECMeasureDelay * 1000) {
   A0V = GetMiddleAnalog();
   if (!Lower && A0V < .18 * MaxAnalog) {
    analogReference(INTERNAL);
    Flush();
    Lower = true;
   }
   if (Lower && A0V > .9 * MaxAnalog) {
    analogReference(DEFAULT);
    Flush();
    Lower = false;
   }
   EC = map(A0V, 0, MaxAnalog, 0, Probe);
   PPM = map(A0V, 0, MaxAnalog, 0, Convert);
   if (Lower) {
    Serial.println("Lower range in use");
    EC = EC * .22;
    PPM = PPM * .22;
   }
   Serial.print("EC = ");
   Serial.println(EC);
   Serial.print("PPM = ");
   Serial.println(PPM);
   Serial.println();
   if (PPM > MaxTDS) {
     digitalWrite(HighECPin,HIGH);
   }
   else {
```

```
      digitalWrite(HighECPin,LOW);
    }
    if (PPM < MinTDS) {
      digitalWrite(LowECPin,HIGH);
    }
    else {
      digitalWrite(LowECPin,LOW);
    }
    PreviousTime = millis();
  }
} //  End main loop

int GetMiddleAnalog(){
  int i, j;
  int n = 5;
  int temp;
  int arr[5];
  digitalWrite(TurnOnSensorPin, HIGH);
  delay(500);
  for (i = 0; i < n; i++){
    arr[i] = analogRead(A0);
    delay(200);
  }
  digitalWrite(TurnOnSensorPin, LOW);
  for (i = 0; i < n; i++){
    for (j = 0; j < n-1; j++) {
      if (arr[j] > arr[j+1]) {
        int temp = arr[j];
        arr[j] = arr[j+1];
        arr[j+1] = temp;
      }
    }
  }
  return arr[2];
}// End GetMiddle

void Flush(){
  int i;
```

```
for (i = 0; i < 10; i++){
  A0V = analogRead(A0);
  delay(5);
  }
}
```
Sketch 8.3

This is a modification of Sketch 8.2. The constant MaxAnalog is simply the maximum value of the analog input. As mentioned before, this is usually 1023, but can occasionally be other values like 4095. Because it appears so often in this sketch, I have made it a defined constant to make it easy to change if necessary. I have added the boolean variable Lower that is true if the Arduino is using the lower range that goes up to 1.1 volts and false if it is using the upper range that goes to 5 volts.

I have added the subroutine Flush. When you change the analogReference of the Arduino, there is a residual charge on the capacitor from the previous setting that can cause erratic readings. Repeatedly reading the analog pin with short delays between readings will flush this charge. At the end of the flush, a valid reading remains in the A0V variable. Since this process is done in two places in the program, I have made it a subroutine.

In the main loop, the statement
if (!Lower && A0V < .18 * MaxAnalog) {
check for two conditions. The first is !Lower, meaning not Lower, which is true if Lower is false. That is, this is checking to see if the Arduino is currently working in the upper range. The second condition is that the analog reading be less than .18 times the maximum reading. This would be .9 volts. If these conditions are both true, the statement
analogReference(INTERNAL);
switches to the internal range of 0 to 1.1 volts. The Flush subroutine is then called, to both flush the capacitor and load a new value into A0V. The variable Lower is then set

to true, to record the fact that the Arduino is now operating in the lower range.

The same process is done to switch to the upper range. The statement

if (Lower && A0V > .9 * MaxAnalog) {

checks to see if the Arduino is currently operating in the lower range and if the A0V reading is over 90% of this range. If these are both true, the statement

analogReference(DEFAULT);

sets the Arduino analog inputs to the default range of 0 to 5 volts. The Flush subroutine is then called, and Lower is set to false.

If the lower range is in effect the

if (Lower) {

condition multiplies the value of EC and TDS by .22. This is because with the maximum analog input range being 1.1 instead of 5, all readings are about 4.545 times as large, so the readings appear too high.

The rest of the sketch is the same as Sketch 8.2.

As I said at the beginning of this chapter, you can also make your own probe if you do not need it to be as accurate as a commercial probe. After all, what you probably really want to know is just if the TDS goes above or below some danger level. If so, you can make a simple probe for a few dollars instead of shelling out $75 or so.

Measuring EC is done by putting two electrodes into the water and applying a small voltage through the water and a reference resistor to measure the electrical conductivity of the water. The electrodes are just two pieces of metal held at a constant distance from each other by a nonconducting material. You can find an object that fits this description, or fashion one on your own. One commonly available object that fits the bill is an electrical plug, as shown in Figure 8.4. You can salvage one from a defunct electrical appliance, or in a worse case, cut one from an inexpensive extension cord. Figure 8.5 shows as simple homemade probe consisting of a piece of plastic with eight holes punched in it. Two wires each go through the holes and are held in place by the holes. There are many other ways you can fix two wires or other pieces of metal a set distance apart, such as driving nails through Styrofoam.

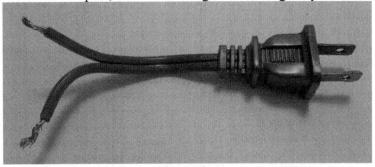

Figure 8.4

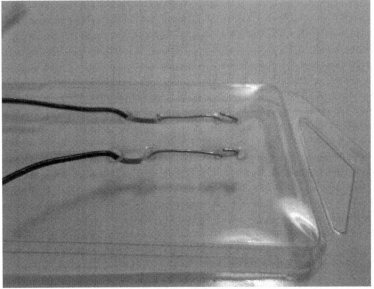

Figure 8.5

I want to make it clear that any such a homemade probe is not as good as the professional ones. They are more subject to error, drift, corrosion, and other problems. It will need to be monitored and recalibrated more often than professional probes. However, if measuring TDS or EC is a minor issue for you and you do not want to spend significant amounts of money on an EC probe, you can follow the directions in the rest of this chapter.

There is a catch to making your own probe. If you continue to run a direct current through the electrodes into the water, the electrodes will quickly become coated with a thin layer of gas (polarized). This will act as electrical insulation, cutting down the current. You can actually watch the readings drop second by second if you continuously run a DC current through the electrodes. To prevent this, you need to use an alternating current to the probe. Commercial probes do this. Normally, Arduinos provide DC. Fortunately, having an Arduino provide an alternating current is not as hard as you might think. Figure 8.6 shows the circuit.

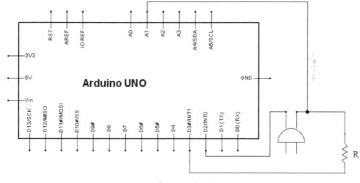

Figure 8.6

You have a simple voltage divider with the resistor and the probe. In this schematic, the voltage across the divider is supplied by digital output pins 2 and 3, but you can use any two output pins you want. By setting pin 2 HIGH and pin 3 LOW for a fraction of a second, taking a reading from the analog input, and then setting pin 2 LOW and pin HIGH for the same amount of time, you provide an alternating current. This prevents the probe contacts from becoming polarized. Between readings, you can set both output pins LOW to prevent any current from flowing. You can also totally disconnect the power from the pins with a relay, which I will discuss later.

The best value of resistor R will depend on your circumstances. The best value is one that matches the resistance of your solution between the probe contacts when the level of dissolved solids in your water is ideal. This will provide the maximum variation in readings as the concentration of dissolved solids in your water varies. If you have an ohmmeter, one simple method of determining this to connect the ohmmeter to the probe and measure the water resistance while the concentration is ideal. If you do not have an ohmmeter, you can construct the circuit, read the analog output, and swap out resistors until the reading is about 500, since that is midway between 0 and 1023. If the reading is high, use a smaller resistor. (Hint: If your ideal TDS is about 10 PPM, I suggest starting with a resistance of 10 K to 22 K.) Sketch 8.4 takes a reading every 2 seconds and sends it to the serial monitor.

```
#define PowerPin1 3
#define PowerPin2 2

int MeasureDelay = 2;
long PreviousTime = 0;
int A1V;

void setup(){
  pinMode(PowerPin1, OUTPUT);
  digitalWrite(PowerPin1, LOW);
  pinMode(PowerPin2, OUTPUT);
  digitalWrite(PowerPin2, LOW);
  Serial.begin(9600);
}// End setup

void loop() {
 if (millis() < PreviousTime) {PreviousTime = 0;}
 if (millis() - PreviousTime >= MeasureDelay * 1000) {
  digitalWrite(PowerPin1, HIGH);
  digitalWrite(PowerPin2, LOW);
  delay(250);
  A1V = analogRead(A1);
  digitalWrite(PowerPin1, LOW);
```

```
    digitalWrite(PowerPin2, HIGH);
    delay(250);
    digitalWrite(PowerPin2, LOW);
    PreviousTime = millis();
    Serial.print("A1 = ");
    Serial.println(A1V);
  }
} // End main loop
```

Sketch 8.4

The first two lines define the pins that will provide the power to the voltage divider. MeasureDelay is the time between readings in seconds. For this sketch, I have set it to two seconds so you can quickly see the readings. In later sketches where you are leaving the device alone, you can set this to a longer period. PreviousTime tracks when the last reading was taken, and A2V is the number from 0 to 1023 that represents voltage at analog input A1.

The setup routine sets the power pins for the voltage divider to output mode and sets them initially to LOW. It also initializes serial communication.

In the main loop, the first if statement resets time of the previous reading to 0 if the millis() function has rolled over. The second if statement checks to see if the time since the last reading is more than the delay period between readings. If it is, the next two lines set power pin 1 to HIGH and power pin 2 to LOW, providing power to the voltage divider. The delay statement waits 250 milliseconds (one half second) before taking the analog reading. This is because the analog inputs each have a small capacitor that needs to charge up to the current voltage level. The next statement takes the analog reading and stores it in A1V. Then the sketch reverses the polarity of the power to the probe contacts for the same length of time to depolarize them. Then both outputs are set to LOW to turn off power to the probe. The statement
PreviousTime = millis();

sets the time of this measurement to the current time. Finally, the Serial.print statements send the readings to the serial monitor.

This sketch is sending the raw reading to the serial monitor to help you select a resistor that gives a reading of about 500 for the proper levels of TDS. You may want to have a sketch convert this raw reading to PPM (parts per million) dissolved solids level. To do this, you will need to calibrate the system. This can be done the same way you calibrated the pH monitor. You can put the probe is three solutions where you have measured the TDS with a simple hand meter.

First, put the probe in a low PPM TDS solution. The best level of PPM for the low concentration sample would be the low level at which you want the Arduino to take some action. Assuming that you currently have your system at the proper level of TDS, you can prepare the low concentration sample by diluting a container of that water somewhat with very pure water. Then you use the serial monitor to send EL## to the Arduino, where ## is the measured PPM TDS of the calibration solution. For example, if the level of TDS of the sample is 5, send EL5 to the Arduino. Next, put the probe in a solution that is the ideal level of TDS. Send EM##, such as EM10, to the Arduino to set the middle TDS number. Finally, put the probe in a solution that is at the high level at which you would like the Arduino to take action. Send EU##, such as EU50, to send the upper TDS number.

Sketch 8.5 allows you to do this, as well as taking action if the readings are too high or low.

```
#include <EEPROM.h>
#define PowerPin1 2
#define PowerPin2 3
#define ECActionPin1 4
#define ECActionPin2 5
#define ECInputPin A2
#define MaxInput 1023
```

```
// Time in minutes between readings
float NormalDelay = 60;
float MeasureDelay = NormalDelay;
// Level of TDS to take action
unsigned int TooLow = 5;
unsigned int TooHigh = 50;
// Time to act
unsigned long OnTime1 = 30;
unsigned long OnTime2 = 60;
float R = 10000;

String CalCommand;
unsigned int CalLowEC = 0;
float CalLowTDS = 0;
unsigned int CalMidEC = 570;
float CalMidTDS = 14;
unsigned int CalHighEC = 863;
float CalHighTDS = 160;
byte HighByte;
byte LowByte;
byte CalStatusEC;
unsigned int TempInt;
unsigned long PreviousTime = 0;
unsigned int EC;
unsigned int TDS;
unsigned int PrevTDS;

void setup(){
  pinMode(PowerPin1, OUTPUT);
  digitalWrite(PowerPin1, LOW);
  pinMode(PowerPin2, OUTPUT);
  digitalWrite(PowerPin2, LOW);
  pinMode(ECActionPin1, OUTPUT);
  digitalWrite(ECActionPin1, LOW);
  Serial.begin(9600);
  CalStatusEC = EEPROM.read(23);
  if (CalStatusEC > 7) {
```

```
    CalStatusEC = 0;
    EEPROM.write(23, CalStatusEC);
  }
  Serial.print("CalStatusEC = ");
  Serial.println(CalStatusEC);
  if ((CalStatusEC & 1) == 1){
    HighByte = EEPROM.read(24);
    LowByte = EEPROM.read(25);
    if (HighByte + LowByte < 510) {
      CalLowEC = (HighByte << 8) + LowByte;
    }
    HighByte = EEPROM.read(26);
    LowByte = EEPROM.read(27);
    if (HighByte + LowByte < 510) {
      TempInt = (HighByte << 8) + LowByte;
      CalLowTDS = TempInt / 100.0;
    }
  }
  Serial.print("Low EC: ");
  Serial.print(CalLowEC);
  Serial.print("   ");
  Serial.println(CalLowTDS);

  if ((CalStatusEC & 2) == 2){
    HighByte = EEPROM.read(28);
    LowByte = EEPROM.read(29);
    if (HighByte + LowByte < 510) {
      CalMidEC = (HighByte << 8) + LowByte;
    }
    HighByte = EEPROM.read(30);
    LowByte = EEPROM.read(31);
    if (HighByte + LowByte < 510) {
      TempInt = (HighByte << 8) + LowByte;
      CalMidTDS = TempInt / 100.0;
    }
  }
  Serial.print("Mid EC: ");
  Serial.print(CalMidEC);
```

```
  Serial.print("  ");
  Serial.println(CalMidTDS);
  if ((CalStatusEC & 4) == 4){
    HighByte = EEPROM.read(32);
    LowByte = EEPROM.read(33);
    if (HighByte + LowByte < 510) {
      CalHighEC = (HighByte << 8) + LowByte;
    }
    HighByte = EEPROM.read(34);
    LowByte = EEPROM.read(35);
    if (HighByte + LowByte < 510) {
      TempInt = (HighByte << 8) + LowByte;
      CalHighTDS = TempInt / 100.0;
    }
  }
  Serial.print("High EC: ");
  Serial.print(CalHighEC);
  Serial.print("  ");
  Serial.println(CalHighTDS);
  Serial.println("");
  for (int n = 0; n < 5; n++) {
   EC = GetMiddleAnalogEC();
   delay(10);
  }
  Serial.println();
}// End setup

void loop() {
   while (Serial.available()) {
     delay(4);  //delay to allow buffer to fill
     if (Serial.available() >0) {
       char c = Serial.read();
       CalCommand += c;
     }
   } //End of while loop that reads string
   if (CalCommand.length() >0){
     CalCommand.toUpperCase();
     Serial.println(CalCommand);
```

```
if (CalCommand.startsWith("EL")) {
  CalCommand = CalCommand.substring(2);
  CalLowTDS = CalCommand.toFloat();
  CalLowEC = GetMiddleAnalogEC();
  CalStatusEC = CalStatusEC | 1;
  EEPROM.write(23, CalStatusEC);
  EEPROM.write(24, highByte(CalLowEC));
  EEPROM.write(25, lowByte(CalLowEC));
  TempInt = CalLowTDS * 100;
  EEPROM.write(26, highByte(TempInt));
  EEPROM.write(27, lowByte(TempInt));
}
if (CalCommand.startsWith("EM")) {
  CalCommand = CalCommand.substring(2);
  CalMidTDS = CalCommand.toFloat();
  CalMidEC = GetMiddleAnalogEC();
  CalStatusEC = CalStatusEC | 2;
  EEPROM.write(23, CalStatusEC);
  EEPROM.write(28, highByte(CalMidEC));
  EEPROM.write(29, lowByte(CalMidEC));
  TempInt = CalMidTDS * 100;
  EEPROM.write(30, highByte(TempInt));
  EEPROM.write(31, lowByte(TempInt));
}
if (CalCommand.startsWith("EU")) {
  CalCommand = CalCommand.substring(2);
  CalHighTDS = CalCommand.toFloat();
  CalHighEC = GetMiddleAnalogEC();
  CalStatusEC = CalStatusEC | 4;
  EEPROM.write(23, CalStatusEC);
  EEPROM.write(32, highByte(CalHighEC));
  EEPROM.write(33, lowByte(CalHighEC));
  TempInt = CalHighTDS * 100.0;
  EEPROM.write(34, highByte(TempInt));
  EEPROM.write(35, lowByte(TempInt));
}
if (CalCommand == "R") {
  GetTDS();
```

```
    }
  CalCommand = "";
  } // End of if (CalCommand.length() >0 )
if (millis() < PreviousTime) {PreviousTime = 0;}
if ((millis() - PreviousTime)/60000.0 >= MeasureDelay) {
  PrevTDS = TDS;
  GetTDS();
  if (TDS < TooLow){
    MeasureDelay = 1;
    Serial.print("Delay = ");
    Serial.println(MeasureDelay);
  }
  if (TDS < TooLow && PrevTDS < TooLow){
    digitalWrite(ECActionPin1, HIGH);
    delay(OnTime1 * 1000);
    digitalWrite(ECActionPin1, LOW);
  }
  else {
    digitalWrite(ECActionPin1, LOW);
  }
  if (TDS > TooHigh){
    MeasureDelay = 1;
    Serial.print("Delay = ");
    Serial.println(MeasureDelay);
  }
  if (TDS > TooHigh & PrevTDS > TooHigh){
    digitalWrite(ECActionPin2, HIGH);
    delay(OnTime2 * 1000);
    digitalWrite(ECActionPin2, LOW);
  }
  else {
    digitalWrite(ECActionPin2, LOW);
  }
  if (TDS > TooLow && TDS < TooHigh) {
    MeasureDelay = NormalDelay;
  }
  PreviousTime = millis();
} // End if testing
```

```
} // End main loop

unsigned int GetMiddleAnalogEC(){
  int i, j;
  const int n = 5;
  int temp;
  int arr[n];
  for (i = 0; i < n; i++){
    digitalWrite(PowerPin1, HIGH);
    digitalWrite(PowerPin2, LOW);
    delay(2);
    arr[i] = analogRead(ECInputPin);
    digitalWrite(PowerPin1, LOW);
    digitalWrite(PowerPin2, HIGH);
    delay(2);
  }
  digitalWrite(PowerPin2, LOW);
  for (i = 0; i < n-1; i++) {
    for (j = 0; j < n-i-1; j++) {
      if (arr[j] > arr[j+1]) {
        int temp = arr[j];
        arr[j] = arr[j+1];
        arr[j+1] = temp;
      }
    }
  }
  float RM = (MaxInput * R / arr[n/2]) - R;
  Serial.print("  A = ");
  Serial.print(arr[n/2]);
  float ECT = (1/RM) * 1E7;
  return ECT;
}// End GetMiddleAnalogEC

void GetTDS() {
  EC = GetMiddleAnalogEC();
  if (EC > CalMidEC) {
```

```
  TDS = CalMidTDS + (CalHighTDS -
CalMidTDS)/(CalHighEC - CalMidEC) *(EC -
CalMidEC);
  }
  if (EC <= CalMidEC) {
   TDS = CalMidTDS - (CalMidTDS -
CalLowTDS)/(CalMidEC - CalLowEC) *(CalMidEC -
EC);
  }
  Serial.print(" EC = ");
  Serial.print(EC);
  Serial.print("   TDS = ");
  Serial.println(TDS);
}
```

Sketch 8.5

This is an extension of Sketch 8.4, with many parts borrowed from Sketch 7.2. I have included the EEPROM library so the program can save the calibration. I have added ECActionPin1 and ECActionPin2 pins to be the pins that will be turned on if the EC (and therefore TDS) becomes too high or low. I have also used a constant to define the analog input pin to allow you to change it more easily later. MaxInput is the highest value that the analog input will read. As I have mentioned before, this is almost always 1023, but can rarely vary or be changed on some Arduinos to values such as 4095, so you can change this here is you have such an Arduino.

NormalDelay is the delay in minutes that you will normally have between readings. MeasureDelay is the actual time between readings. As I will explain shortly, the code can change the time between readings to suit circumstances. I have changed time period given in Sketch 8.4 for these from seconds to minutes and made it a float variable so it can be fractions. In Sketch 8.4, the purpose was to report to you the raw readings quickly so you could choose a resistor. In Sketch 8.5, you will probably want to test the TDS much less frequently, because it probably will not change often. Therefore, I have set it to 60 minutes, although you can set it for whatever you want.

TooLow and TooHigh are the levels of TDS that you want the Arduino to take action, specifically setting the output pins high to turn on an alarm, a filter, a device to add nutrients, or whatever you decide. OnTime1 is the amount of time in seconds you want the Arduino to take action, such as pump in nutrients, if the TDS gets too low. OnTime2 is the amount of time in seconds you want the Arduino to take action, such as run a filter, if the TDS gets too high. I will discuss how to make this indefinitely shortly. R is the value of the resistor you have in your circuit. I have found that 10000 (a 10K resistor) works well in my tests, but as explained above, you will need to select a value that suits your circumstances, and you must assign this value to R on the code.

CalLowEC, CalLowTDS, CalMidEC, CalMidTDS, CalHighEC, and CalHighTDS are the variables used to convert the raw analog input readings to TDS measurements in PPM. CalLowEC is the raw reading for the lower calibration point, and CalLowTDS is the equivalent TDS in PPM. Likewise, CalMidEC is the raw reading for the middle calibration point and CalMidTDS is the equivalent TDS. CalHighEC and CalHighTDS are the raw and equivalent values for the high point. CalStatusEC is the status of the calibration, and stores how many calibration points have been calibrated so far. It is the same thing as CalStatus in the previous chapter. PreviousTime is the time the previous reading was taken, EC is the EC reading, and TDS is the value you get after the conversion.

The setup routine is the same as the one in Sketch 7.2, except the variable names and memory addresses have been changed. As in Sketch 7.2, it reads stored conversion values from memory. I have increased every memory location by 20, so you could use the same Arduino for this as for reading the pH. However, reading the TDS interferes with the process of reading the pH, and vice versa, so precautions must be taken to make sure you never read them both at the same time. I will discuss these later. I have also added a for loop that calls the GetMiddleAnalogEC() function several times, because sometimes the first few initial readings are off a bit.

I have added the same type of subroutine for taking the middle analog reading as in Sketch 7.2, and named it GetMiddleAnalogEC. However, it is more complicated because of the need to reverse the polarity of the electrodes to avoid polarization. First, it sets PowerPin1 HIGH and PowerPin2 LOW and delays 200 milliseconds. Then it takes the five readings, with a 20 millisecond delay between each reading. Then it sets PowerPin1 LOW and PowerPin2 HIGH and delays 300 milliseconds to reverse the polarization. Then it sorts the values obtained from low to high so the middle value can easily be found, as was done in Sketch 7.2. Next, it converts the value read from the analog pin to electrical conductivity. The line
float RM = (MaxInput * R / arr[2]) - R;
calculates the measured resistance of the water from the analog reading and stores it in the variable RM (Resistance Measured). Conductivity is the inverse of resistance, so the line
float ECT = (1/RM) * 1E7
converts the resistance to conductivity and stores it in ECT (EC temporary). The part of this line that reads "* 1E7" merely multiples the value by 10 to the seventh power in order to increase the value to well over 1, so that it can be stored as an integer when it is stored in memory.

I have added a subroutine, GetTDS(), that the code can call to calculate the TDS. This is because in the code I have created several points that ask for the TDS, so putting that in a subroutine saves writing the same code in several places. This subroutine called the GetMiddleAnalogEC() function and stores the result in EC. The next few lines convert the raw analog value to a TDS PPM value. If the reading is greater than the middle value (EC > CalMidEC), it uses one equation. If it is less than or equal to the middle value, it uses another. It sends the values of both EC and

TDS to the serial port, in addition to providing them to the rest of the program. Note that since EC and TDS are defined in the main body of the code at the beginning, it is not necessary to return them as a value. Simply setting them within the subroutine sets the values for the entire program.

In the main loop, I start off with the same code to input a command from the serial port that I used in Sketch 7.2 and use it to calibrate the system. First, the
while (Serial.available())
loop builds a string if characters are incoming from the serial port. Then, if a string has been built (if CalCommand.length() >0), there are three if statements that check to see if the string starts with EL, EM, or EU, respectively. If so, each if function strips off the first two characters, converts the remainder to a numeric value, uses the GetMiddleAnalogEC subroutine to get the current analog reading, and stores the two values in EEPROM memory locations.

There is also one if statement that looks for a serial input of the single letter R. If it receives this, it calls the GetTDS() subroutine. You can use this to force the Arduino to deliver the measurements of EC and TDS to you at any time, without waiting for the set delay time to pass.

The statement
if (millis() < PreviousTime) {PreviousTime = 0;}
adjusts the PreviousTime variable if the millis() function has rolled over. The statement
if ((millis() - PreviousTime)/60000.0 >= MeasureDelay)
checks to see if the amount of time MeasureDelay has passed since the previous reading. It divides the time period millis() - PreviousTime by 60000.0 to convert the milliseconds to minutes. Notice the point zero at the end. This tells the Arduino to use floating point calculations and return a decimal value. Without that point zero, the Arduino would use integer arithmetic and round the answer to the nearest whole number, because all of the values involved would be integers.

If the time period has passed, the code stores the value of TDS in PrevTDS. It then calls the GetTDS() subroutine to get the values of EC and TDS. By storing the value of TDS in PrevTDS before getting an updated value of TDS, it now has a record of the current and most recent previous value. This will be a safety precaution to prevent the Arduino from acting on a single reading.

Next, it checks to see if TDS is below the TooLow value. If so, it resets the time delay between readings to one minute. This will cause the Arduino to wait one minute and then take another reading. If both readings are below TooLow, then both TDS and PrevTDS will be below TooLow. If that happens, the line
if (TDS < TooLow && PrevTDS < TooLow){
is true and the next lines set ActionPin1 HIGH, then delay for OnTime1 seconds, then sets ActionPin1 LOW. This allows you to have a pump add nutrients for a set number of seconds, or some similar action. If you are just having it turn on an alarm or some other action that you want to keep on until the TDS levels change, delete the lines
delay(OnTime1 * 1000);
digitalWrite(ActionPin1, LOW);
from the code.

The else statement turns off ActionPin1 if the TDS levels have risen above the threshold. This is redundant and has no effect if you leave in the statement to turn off the pin after a set delay, but I have included it to turn off ActionPin1 once TDS levels have risen if you have deleted those lines.

The exact same action occurs if the TDS levels are too high (TDS > TooHigh). Again, you can delete the lines
delay(OnTime2 * 1000);
digitalWrite(ActionPin2, LOW);
if you want the action to continue until the TDS levels return to normal, such as if you are sounding an alarm.

The statements
if (TDS > TooLow && TDS < TooHigh) {
  MeasureDelay = NormalDelay;

```
    Serial.print("Delay = ");
    Serial.println(MeasureDelay);
}
```
restore the time between measurements to the longer time once normal TDS levels have been restored.

The statement
```
PreviousTime = millis();
```
sets the time of the test to the current time so the Arduino can start counting to the next test. Note that this happens after everything is done, not immediately after the current reading is actually taken. Therefore, the time to the next test starts after any delays created by the code. This is important, because if PreviousTime had been set in the code right after the measurement was actually taken and you set MeasureDelay to 1 (as I did in this example) and OnTime1 or OnTime2 to more than 60 seconds, the next test would occur immediately.

As you may recall, when EC measurements are not being taken, the Sketches 8.4 and 8.5 set the pins powering the probe to LOW. This stops the test, but it does leave an active connection to the Arduino ground (GND) in the water. This can interfere with some other tests, because it would allow current to flow through the water from another test instrument to the Arduino ground. Examples of instruments that this can cause problems with would be a pH probe or another EC probe if you have two in the water. This might not be a problem if you have a separate Arduino conducting each measurement, but you might want to have one Arduino conducting several tests. Therefore, it is good to have the option to totally disconnect the probe from any power. You can do this with a relay. Figure 8.7 shows how to do this.

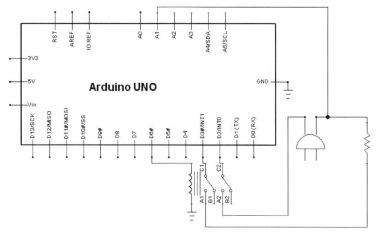

Figure 8.7

This adds a relay that only connects the probe to the output pins when it is turned on, which happens when output pin 6 is HIGH. The schematic shows a DPDT relay. You can use a DPST normally open relay if you want, but most relays designed for Arduinos are DTDP. Sketch 8.6 includes the code to do this.

```
#include <EEPROM.h>
#define PowerPin1 2
#define PowerPin2 3
#define ECActionPin1 4
#define ECActionPin2 5
#define ECPowerOn 6
#define ECInputPin A2
#define MaxInput 1023


// Time in minutes between readings
float NormalDelay = 60;
float MeasureDelay = NormalDelay;
// Level of TDS to take action
unsigned int TooLow = 5;
unsigned int TooHigh = 50;
// Time to act
```

173

```
unsigned long OnTime1 = 30;
unsigned long OnTime2 = 60;
float R = 10000;

String CalCommand;
unsigned int CalLowEC = 0;
float CalLowTDS = 0;
unsigned int CalMidEC = 570;
float CalMidTDS = 14;
unsigned int CalHighEC = 863;
float CalHighTDS = 160;
byte HighByte;
byte LowByte;
byte CalStatusEC;
unsigned int TempInt;
unsigned long PreviousTime = 0;
unsigned int EC;
unsigned int TDS;
unsigned int PrevTDS;

void setup(){
  pinMode(PowerPin1, OUTPUT);
  digitalWrite(PowerPin1, LOW);
  pinMode(PowerPin2, OUTPUT);
  digitalWrite(PowerPin2, LOW);
  pinMode(ECActionPin1, OUTPUT);
  digitalWrite(ECActionPin1, LOW);
  pinMode(ECPowerOn, OUTPUT);
  digitalWrite(ECPowerOn, LOW);
  Serial.begin(9600);
  CalStatusEC = EEPROM.read(23);
  if (CalStatusEC > 7) {
   CalStatusEC = 0;
   EEPROM.write(23, CalStatusEC);
  }
  Serial.print("CalStatusEC = ");
  Serial.println(CalStatusEC);
  if ((CalStatusEC & 1) == 1){
```

```
    HighByte = EEPROM.read(24);
    LowByte = EEPROM.read(25);
    if (HighByte + LowByte < 510) {
      CalLowEC = (HighByte << 8) + LowByte;
    }
    HighByte = EEPROM.read(26);
    LowByte = EEPROM.read(27);
    if (HighByte + LowByte < 510) {
      TempInt = (HighByte << 8) + LowByte;
      CalLowTDS = TempInt / 100.0;
    }
  }
  Serial.print("Low EC: ");
  Serial.print(CalLowEC);
  Serial.print("   ");
  Serial.println(CalLowTDS);

  if ((CalStatusEC & 2) == 2){
    HighByte = EEPROM.read(28);
    LowByte = EEPROM.read(29);
    if (HighByte + LowByte < 510) {
      CalMidEC = (HighByte << 8) + LowByte;
    }
    HighByte = EEPROM.read(30);
    LowByte = EEPROM.read(31);
    if (HighByte + LowByte < 510) {
      TempInt = (HighByte << 8) + LowByte;
      CalMidTDS = TempInt / 100.0;
    }
  }
  Serial.print("Mid EC: ");
  Serial.print(CalMidEC);
  Serial.print("   ");
  Serial.println(CalMidTDS);
  if ((CalStatusEC & 4) == 4){
    HighByte = EEPROM.read(32);
    LowByte = EEPROM.read(33);
    if (HighByte + LowByte < 510) {
```

```
    CalHighEC = (HighByte << 8) + LowByte;
  }
  HighByte = EEPROM.read(34);
  LowByte = EEPROM.read(35);
  if (HighByte + LowByte < 510) {
    TempInt = (HighByte << 8) + LowByte;
    CalHighTDS = TempInt / 100.0;
  }
 }
 Serial.print("High EC: ");
 Serial.print(CalHighEC);
 Serial.print("   ");
 Serial.println(CalHighTDS);
 Serial.println("");
 for (int n = 0; n < 5; n++) {
  EC = GetMiddleAnalogEC();
  delay(10);
 }
 Serial.println();
}// End setup

void loop() {
   while (Serial.available()) {
     delay(4);  //delay to allow buffer to fill
     if (Serial.available() >0) {
       char c = Serial.read();
       CalCommand += c;
     }
   } //End of while loop that reads string
   if (CalCommand.length() >0){
    CalCommand.toUpperCase();
    Serial.println(CalCommand);
    if (CalCommand.startsWith("EL")) {
     CalCommand = CalCommand.substring(2);
     CalLowTDS = CalCommand.toFloat();
     CalLowEC = GetMiddleAnalogEC();
     CalStatusEC = CalStatusEC | 1;
     EEPROM.write(23, CalStatusEC);
```

```
      EEPROM.write(24, highByte(CalLowEC));
      EEPROM.write(25, lowByte(CalLowEC));
      TempInt = CalLowTDS * 100;
      EEPROM.write(26, highByte(TempInt));
      EEPROM.write(27, lowByte(TempInt));
    }
    if (CalCommand.startsWith("EM")) {
      CalCommand = CalCommand.substring(2);
      CalMidTDS = CalCommand.toFloat();
      CalMidEC = GetMiddleAnalogEC();
      CalStatusEC = CalStatusEC | 2;
      EEPROM.write(23, CalStatusEC);
      EEPROM.write(28, highByte(CalMidEC));
      EEPROM.write(29, lowByte(CalMidEC));
      TempInt = CalMidTDS * 100;
      EEPROM.write(30, highByte(TempInt));
      EEPROM.write(31, lowByte(TempInt));
    }
    if (CalCommand.startsWith("EU")) {
      CalCommand = CalCommand.substring(2);
      CalHighTDS = CalCommand.toFloat();
      CalHighEC = GetMiddleAnalogEC();
      CalStatusEC = CalStatusEC | 4;
      EEPROM.write(23, CalStatusEC);
      EEPROM.write(32, highByte(CalHighEC));
      EEPROM.write(33, lowByte(CalHighEC));
      TempInt = CalHighTDS * 100.0;
      EEPROM.write(34, highByte(TempInt));
      EEPROM.write(35, lowByte(TempInt));
    }
    if (CalCommand == "R") {
      GetTDS();
    }
    CalCommand = "";
  } // End of if (CalCommand.length() >0)
  if (millis() < PreviousTime) {PreviousTime = 0;}
  if ((millis() - PreviousTime)/60000.0 >= MeasureDelay) {
    PrevTDS = TDS;
```

```
    GetTDS();
    if (TDS < TooLow){
      MeasureDelay = 1;
      Serial.print("Delay = ");
      Serial.println(MeasureDelay);
    }
    if (TDS < TooLow && PrevTDS < TooLow){
      digitalWrite(ECActionPin1, HIGH);
      delay(OnTime1 * 1000);
      digitalWrite(ECActionPin1, LOW);
    }
    else {
      digitalWrite(ECActionPin1, LOW);
    }
    if (TDS > TooHigh){
      MeasureDelay = 1;
      Serial.print("Delay = ");
      Serial.println(MeasureDelay);
    }
    if (TDS > TooHigh & PrevTDS > TooHigh){
      digitalWrite(ECActionPin2, HIGH);
      delay(OnTime2 * 1000);
      digitalWrite(ECActionPin2, LOW);
    }
    else {
      digitalWrite(ECActionPin2, LOW);
    }
    if (TDS > TooLow && TDS < TooHigh) {
      MeasureDelay = NormalDelay;
    }
    PreviousTime = millis();
  } // End if testing
} //  End main loop

unsigned int GetMiddleAnalogEC(){
  int i, j;
  const int n = 5;
  int temp;
```

```
  int arr[n];
  digitalWrite(ECPowerOn, HIGH);
  delay(500);
  for (i = 0; i < n; i++){
    digitalWrite(PowerPin1, HIGH);
    digitalWrite(PowerPin2, LOW);
    delay(2);
    arr[i] = analogRead(ECInputPin);
    digitalWrite(PowerPin1, LOW);
    digitalWrite(PowerPin2, HIGH);
    delay(2);
  }
  digitalWrite(PowerPin2, LOW);
  digitalWrite(ECPowerOn, LOW);
  for (i = 0; i < n-1; i++) {
    for (j = 0; j < n-i-1; j++) {
      if (arr[j] > arr[j+1]) {
        int temp = arr[j];
        arr[j] = arr[j+1];
        arr[j+1] = temp;
      }
    }
  }
  float RM = (MaxInput * R / arr[n/2]) - R;
  Serial.print("  A = ");
  Serial.print(arr[n/2]);
  float ECT = (1/RM) * 1E7;
  return ECT;
}// End GetMiddleAnalogEC

void GetTDS() {
  EC = GetMiddleAnalogEC();
  if (EC > CalMidEC) {
    TDS = CalMidTDS + (CalHighTDS - CalMidTDS)/(CalHighEC - CalMidEC) *(EC - CalMidEC);
  }
  if (EC <= CalMidEC) {
```

```
   TDS = CalMidTDS - (CalMidTDS -
CalLowTDS)/(CalMidEC - CalLowEC) *(CalMidEC -
EC);
  }
  Serial.print(" EC = ");
  Serial.print(EC);
  Serial.print("   TDS = ");
  Serial.println(TDS);
}
```

Sketch 8.6

This really only adds six lines of code. The cut off pin is defined, the setup routine defines this pin as output and sets it low initially. The GetMiddleAnalogEC subroutine turns it on and delays 100 milliseconds to allow the relay contacts to close before taking a reading, and then turns it off again after taking the reading.

One problem with measuring TDS is that the measurement can be affected by temperature. As temperature goes up, the reading will go up, even if the actual TDS PPM is really the same. This is because the ions become more active as the temperature goes up. The amount that the reading will go up is the temperature correction coefficient of electrical conductivity. It is generally about 2% per degree Celsius. For example, if the water temperature goes up 5 degrees C, the reading will change about 10%. However, but it does vary. The coefficient can be different depending on precisely what the dissolved solids are, what their concentrations are, and the temperature. Because of these factors, trying to compensate for the temperature is not entirely reliable.

However, it is possible to at least a partially compensate for temperature. The equation is
$TDSA = TDS/(1 + (C/100) * (T - TO))$,
where TDSA is TDS adjusted for temperature, TDS is the current measured value without compensating for temperature, C is the coefficient, T is the current temperature, and TO is the original temperature the meter is

calibrated at. The idea is that if you calibrated the meter at temperature TO and got reading TDS and then take a reading of the same solution at temperature T, this equation should convert the second reading to the first. As I said, the effect is not perfect because so many factors are not linear, but it will be closer than if you had not compensated at all.

To compensate for temperature effects on TDS readings, it is necessary to have both the water temperature thermometer and the EC probe on the same Arduino. Fortunately, these do not conflict at all. I did this and conducted some experiments to determine the effectiveness. In my experiments, I used a jar of water with a TDS of 93 and calibrated it at 23.56 C (74.41 F). I then heated the solution to 50.56 C (123 F) and retested it. The measured TDS was 171.54. The adjusted TDS was 101.76. Not the correct value of 93, but definitely a lot closer. This was, of course, an extreme test, since if the water gets to 123 F, your system has a lot more problems that the TDS level. As the temperature cooled, the adjusted TDS measurement got progressively closer to the correct value. By the time the temperature got down to 33.5 C (92.3 F), the measured TDS was 118.8 and the adjusted TDS was 94.7, as reasonably small error from 93, especially compared to 118.8. When I refrigerated the solution down to 12.69 C (54.84 F), the measured TDS was 71.1, but the adjusted TDS was 92.96, essentially exactly right.

Sketch 8.7 adjusts the TDS reading for temperature.

```
#include <EEPROM.h>
#include <OneWire.h>
#include <DallasTemperature.h>

#define PowerPin1 2
#define PowerPin2 3
#define ECActionPin1 4
#define ECActionPin2 5
#define ECPowerOn 6
#define ONE_WIRE_BUS 7
```

```
#define ECInputPin A2
#define MaxInput 1023
#define HeaterPin 13
#define CoolerPin 12
const float TempUpperLimit = 85;
const float TempLowerLimit = 40;

// Time in minutes between readings
float NormalDelay = 60;
float MeasureDelay = NormalDelay;
// Level of TDS to take action
unsigned int TDSTooLow = 5;
unsigned int TDSTooHigh = 50;
// Time to act
unsigned long OnTime1 = 30;
unsigned long OnTime2 = 60;
float R = 10000;

float TempCoef = 2;
unsigned int CalLowEC = 0;
float CalLowTDS = 0;
unsigned int CalMidEC = 570;
float CalMidTDS = 14;
unsigned int CalHighEC = 863;
float CalHighTDS = 160;
byte HighByte;
byte LowByte;
byte CalStatusEC;
unsigned int TempInt;
unsigned long PreviousTime = 0;
String CalCommand;

float EC;
float TDS;
float tempC;
float tempF;
float RefTemp;
float EA;
```

```
float ES;
float TDSA;
float ECA;
unsigned int PrevTDSA;

OneWire oneWire(ONE_WIRE_BUS);
DallasTemperature sensors(&oneWire);

void setup(){
  pinMode(PowerPin1, OUTPUT);
  digitalWrite(PowerPin1, LOW);
  pinMode(PowerPin2, OUTPUT);
  digitalWrite(PowerPin2, LOW);
  pinMode(ECActionPin1, OUTPUT);
  digitalWrite(ECActionPin1, LOW);
  pinMode(ECPowerOn, OUTPUT);
  digitalWrite(ECPowerOn, LOW);
  Serial.begin(9600);
  CalStatusEC = EEPROM.read(23);
  if (CalStatusEC > 7) {
   CalStatusEC = 0;
   EEPROM.write(23, CalStatusEC);
  }
  Serial.print("CalStatusEC = ");
  Serial.println(CalStatusEC);
  if ((CalStatusEC & 1) == 1){
    Serial.println("Reading Low");
    HighByte = EEPROM.read(24);
    LowByte = EEPROM.read(25);
    if (HighByte + LowByte < 510) {
     CalLowEC = (HighByte << 8) + LowByte;
    }
   HighByte = EEPROM.read(26);
   LowByte = EEPROM.read(27);
   if (HighByte + LowByte < 510) {
      TempInt = (HighByte << 8) + LowByte;
      CalLowTDS = TempInt / 100.0;
   }
```

```
}
Serial.print("Low EC: ");
Serial.print(CalLowEC);
Serial.print("   ");
Serial.println(CalLowTDS);
if ((CalStatusEC & 2) == 2){
  Serial.println("Reading Mid");
  HighByte = EEPROM.read(21);
  LowByte = EEPROM.read(22);
  TempInt = (HighByte << 8) + LowByte;
  RefTemp = TempInt / 100.0;
  Serial.print("Reference Temp = ");
  Serial.println(RefTemp);
  HighByte = EEPROM.read(28);
  LowByte = EEPROM.read(29);
  if (HighByte + LowByte < 510) {
    CalMidEC = (HighByte << 8) + LowByte;
  }
  HighByte = EEPROM.read(30);
  LowByte = EEPROM.read(31);
  if (HighByte + LowByte < 510) {
    TempInt = (HighByte << 8) + LowByte;
    CalMidTDS = TempInt / 100.0;
  }
}
Serial.print("Mid EC: ");
Serial.print(CalMidEC);
Serial.print("   ");
Serial.println(CalMidTDS);
if ((CalStatusEC & 4) == 4){
  //Serial.println("Reading High");
  HighByte = EEPROM.read(32);
  LowByte = EEPROM.read(33);
  if (HighByte + LowByte < 510) {
    CalHighEC = (HighByte << 8) + LowByte;
  }
  HighByte = EEPROM.read(34);
  LowByte = EEPROM.read(35);
```

```
    if (HighByte + LowByte < 510) {
      TempInt = (HighByte << 8) + LowByte;
      CalHighTDS = TempInt / 100.0;
     }
   }
   Serial.print("High EC: ");
   Serial.print(CalHighEC);
   Serial.print("   ");
   Serial.println(CalHighTDS);
   sensors.begin();
   for (int n = 0; n < 5; n++) {
   EC = GetMiddleAnalogEC();
   Serial.println();
   delay(10);
   }
 }// End setup

 void loop() {
   sensors.requestTemperatures();
   tempC = sensors.getTempCByIndex(0);
   tempF = (tempC * 1.8) + 32.0;
     while (Serial.available()) {
       delay(4);  //delay to allow buffer to fill
       if (Serial.available() >0) {
         char c = Serial.read();
         CalCommand += c;
       }
     } //End of while loop that reads string
     if (CalCommand.length() >0){
       CalCommand.toUpperCase();
       Serial.println(CalCommand);
       if (CalCommand.startsWith("EL")) {
         CalCommand = CalCommand.substring(2);
         CalLowTDS = CalCommand.toFloat();
         CalLowEC = GetMiddleAnalogEC();
         CalStatusEC = CalStatusEC | 1;
         EEPROM.write(23, CalStatusEC);
         EEPROM.write(24, highByte(CalLowEC));
```

```
    EEPROM.write(25, lowByte(CalLowEC));
    TempInt = CalLowTDS * 100;
    EEPROM.write(26, highByte(TempInt));
    EEPROM.write(27, lowByte(TempInt));
  }
  if (CalCommand.startsWith("EM")) {
    RefTemp = tempC;
    CalCommand = CalCommand.substring(2);
    CalMidTDS = CalCommand.toFloat();
    CalMidEC = GetMiddleAnalogEC();
    CalStatusEC = CalStatusEC | 2;
    TempInt = RefTemp * 100;
    EEPROM.write(21, highByte(TempInt));
    EEPROM.write(22, lowByte(TempInt));
    EEPROM.write(23, CalStatusEC);
    EEPROM.write(28, highByte(CalMidEC));
    EEPROM.write(29, lowByte(CalMidEC));
    TempInt = CalMidTDS * 100;
    EEPROM.write(30, highByte(TempInt));
    EEPROM.write(31, lowByte(TempInt));
  }
  if (CalCommand.startsWith("EU")) {
    CalCommand = CalCommand.substring(2);
    CalHighTDS = CalCommand.toFloat();
    CalHighEC = GetMiddleAnalogEC();
    CalStatusEC = CalStatusEC | 4;
    EEPROM.write(23, CalStatusEC);
    EEPROM.write(32, highByte(CalHighEC));
    EEPROM.write(33, lowByte(CalHighEC));
    TempInt = CalHighTDS * 100.0;
    EEPROM.write(34, highByte(TempInt));
    EEPROM.write(35, lowByte(TempInt));
  }
  if (CalCommand == "R") {
    GetTDS();
  }
  CalCommand = "";
} // End of if (CalCommand.length() >0)
```

```
if (millis() < PreviousTime) {PreviousTime = 0;}
if ((millis() - PreviousTime)/60000.0 >= MeasureDelay) {
 PrevTDSA = TDSA;
 GetTDS();
 if (TDSA < TDSTooLow){
   MeasureDelay = 1;
   Serial.print("Delay = ");
   Serial.println(MeasureDelay);
  }
  if (TDSA < TDSTooLow && PrevTDSA < TDSTooLow){
    digitalWrite(ECActionPin1, HIGH);
    delay(OnTime1 * 1000);
    digitalWrite(ECActionPin1, LOW);
  }
  else {
    digitalWrite(ECActionPin1, LOW);
  }
  if (TDSA > TDSTooHigh){
    MeasureDelay = 1;
    Serial.print("Delay = ");
    Serial.println(MeasureDelay);
  }
  if (TDSA > TDSTooHigh && PrevTDSA > TDSTooHigh){
    digitalWrite(ECActionPin2, HIGH);
    delay(OnTime2 * 1000);
    digitalWrite(ECActionPin2, LOW);
  }
  else {
    digitalWrite(ECActionPin2, LOW);
  }
  if (TDSA > TDSTooLow && TDSA < TDSTooHigh) {
    MeasureDelay = NormalDelay;
  }
 if (tempF < TempLowerLimit) {
   digitalWrite(HeaterPin, HIGH);
```

```
    }
  if (tempF > TempLowerLimit + 3) {
    digitalWrite(HeaterPin, LOW);
    }

  if (tempF > TempUpperLimit){
    digitalWrite(CoolerPin, HIGH);
    }
  if (tempF < TempUpperLimit - 3){
    digitalWrite(CoolerPin, LOW);
    }
    PreviousTime = millis();
  } // End if testing
} //  End main loop

float GetMiddleAnalogEC(){
  int i, j;
  const int n = 5;
  int temp;
  int arr[n];
  digitalWrite(ECPowerOn, HIGH);
  delay(500);
  for (i = 0; i < n; i++){
    digitalWrite(PowerPin1, HIGH);
    digitalWrite(PowerPin2, LOW);
    delay(2);
    arr[i] = analogRead(ECInputPin);
    digitalWrite(PowerPin1, LOW);
    digitalWrite(PowerPin2, HIGH);
    delay(2);
  }
  digitalWrite(PowerPin2, LOW);
  digitalWrite(ECPowerOn, LOW);
  for (i = 0; i < n-1; i++)  {
    for (j = 0; j < n-i-1; j++)  {
      if (arr[j] > arr[j+1]) {
        int temp = arr[j];
        arr[j] = arr[j+1];
```

```
    arr[j+1] = temp;
   }
  }
 }
 float RM = (MaxInput * R / arr[n/2]) - R;
 float ECT = (1/RM) * 1E7;
 return ECT;
}// End GetMiddleAnalogEC

void GetTDS() {
 Serial.print("Temperature = ");
 Serial.print(tempC);
 Serial.println(" C");
 EC = GetMiddleAnalogEC();
 ECA = EC/(1.0 + ((TempCoef/100.0) * (tempC - RefTemp)));
 if (ECA > CalMidEC) {
  TDSA = CalMidTDS + (CalHighTDS - CalMidTDS)/(CalHighEC - CalMidEC) *(ECA - CalMidEC);
 }
 if (ECA <= CalMidEC) {
  TDSA = CalMidTDS - (CalMidTDS - CalLowTDS)/(CalMidEC - CalLowEC) *(CalMidEC - ECA);
 }
 Serial.print("  ECA = ");
 Serial.print(ECA);
 Serial.print("  TDSA = ");
 Serial.println(TDSA);
}
```

Sketch 8.7

Here I have combined Sketch 8.6 and 4.1 (water temperature sensor), and allowed the temperature reading to adjust the TDS reading. Although the point of this exercise is to have the temperature reading adjust the TDS reading, I have left in the parts of Sketch 4.1 that cause the

Arduino to take action if the temperature gets too high or low. Thus, we have a design that reacts to both temperature and TDS being too low or high. Being able to combine functions like this, or like the automatic adjustment of flood and drain to air temperature and humidity, is one of the big advantages to automating an aquaponic or hydroponic system with an Arduino.

In this sketch, I have renamed some of the variables to make it clearer which sensor they refer to. For example, I have changed the names ActionPin1 and ActionPin2 to ECActionPin1 and ECActionPin2 to clarify that they refer to action taken in response to EC measurements, TooLow and TooHigh to TDSTooLow and TDSTooHigh, and so on. TempCoef is the temperature coefficient. RefTemp is the reference temperature at which the EC meter is calibrated (T0 in the equation above). TDSA is TDS adjusted and ECA is EC adjusted.

In the main loop, I have added the code from Sketch 4.1 that inputs the temperature reading from the thermometer sensor. In the part that calibrates the EC to TDS conversion for the middle level (the EM# command from the serial monitor), I have added the following lines.

```
RefTemp = tempC;
TempInt = RefTemp * 100;
EEPROM.write(21, highByte(TempInt));
EEPROM.write(22, lowByte(TempInt));
```

These save the current temperature in the variable RefTemp and store it in memory. Thus, the Arduino has a record of what the temperature was when the system was calibrated, and can compensate for this when it takes a new measurement. In the setup routine, the lines
```
HighByte = EEPROM.read(21);
LowByte = EEPROM.read(22);
TempInt = (HighByte << 8) + LowByte;
RefTemp = TempInt / 100.0;
```

retrieve this reference temperature when the Arduino boots up again if it is turned off.

In the GetTDS() subroutine, it calls GetMiddleAnalogEC() and stores the value in EC as it did in Sketch 8.6. However, immediately after getting the EC reading, the line
ECA = EC/(1.0 + ((TempCoef/100.0) * (tempC - RefTemp)));
calculates the adjusted EC, ECA. It then calculates the adjusted TDS value, TDSA, from ECA. The rest of the sketch performs the same operations based on TDS readings as Sketch 8.3, except it uses the adjusted value TDSA instead of the TDS value that had not been adjusted for temperature.

Note: I have mentioned that you should never test for pH and EC at the same time using the same Arduino. Because of this, I provided functions like
digitalWrite(TurnOffSensorPin, HIGH);
to turn off power to the pH meter to the sketches in the chapter on testing pH and
digitalWrite(ECPowerOn, HIGH);
to turn on power to the EC probe in this chapter. If you do combine the two functions in one sketch, you should put the lines
digitalWrite(TurnOffSensorPin, HIGH);
PHEnabled = false;
delay(1000);
immediately before
digitalWrite(ECPowerOn, HIGH);
in the sketches in this chapter and
delay(500);
digitalWrite(TurnOffSensorPin, LOW);
PHEnabled = true;
after the line
digitalWrite(ECPowerOn, LOW);
This will turn the pH meter off before you apply power to the EC probe and turn it back on when you turn off the EC probe.

In the previous chapter on pH, I suggested including code to cut off any pumping of acid or base if the readings were so unreasonably high or low that they were likely to be a malfunction of the sensor, rather than an actual reading. This was to protect against the system pumping damaging amounts of acid or base into the water due to a malfunction of the sensor. If you are going to have your system automatically adjust the TDS levels, the same could be a good idea for the sketches in this chapter. A short circuit, broken connection, the sensor coming out of the water, or various other conditions could cause extreme inaccurate readings that would not change regardless of the actual EC or TDS.

To prevent this, you can define high and low values that would never actually happen in the beginning of the sketch, such as

unsigned int ErrorReadingLow = 2;
unsigned int ErrorReadingHigh = 100;

These are both arbitrary numbers for demonstration. For your system, you want to make them significantly lower and higher than the low and high levels at which your system triggers adjustments, so they will be readings that your system should never be able to reach. You can also set a pin to be an error alarm, by defining an ErrorAlarmPin in the beginning and setting it to output in the setup routine.

You can then insert the following code just before the code that actually executes adjustments (turns on pins to raise or lower TDS).

if (PPM < ErrorReadingLow || PPM > ErrorReadingHigh){
    digitalWrite(ErrorAlarmPin, HIGH);
}
else {
    digitalWrite(ErrorAlarmPin, LOW);

For example, in Sketch 8.2, you would put the above code just before the line
if (PPM > MaxTDS) {

You would put the closing } bracket just after the last line of code that adjusts the TDS. That section of code would look like this

```
if (PPM < ErrorReadingLow || PPM > ErrorReadingHigh){
  digitalWrite(ErrorAlarmPin, HIGH);
  }
else {
  digitalWrite(ErrorAlarmPin, LOW);
  if (PPM > MaxTDS) {
    digitalWrite(HighECPin,HIGH);
  }
  else {
    digitalWrite(HighECPin,LOW);
  }
  if (PPM < MinTDS) {
    digitalWrite(LowECPin,HIGH);
  }
  else {
    digitalWrite(LowECPin,LOW);
  }
}
```

The effect of this is to turn on the alarm pin if an unrealistic reading occurs. You can attach an LED in series with a resistor or other indicator to the pin to inform you if a malfunction occurs. This is optional, of course, but a worthwhile idea to inform you if there is a problem with the sensor. If the reading is reasonable, the else statement turns off the alarm pin and then allows the sketch to make the tests to see if the readings warrant taking action.

You would make slight modifications to the error testing code for the other sketches. For example, in Sketch 8.5 or 8.6 you would use TDS instead of PPP, so the line would read
if (TDS < ErrorReadingLow || TDS > ErrorReadingHigh){
In Sketch 8.7 you would use TDSA.

Chapter 9

Turbidity

One sign of trouble in any fish tank is sudden turbidity (cloudiness) of the water. A sudden increase in turbidity can indicate several conditions, such as a sudden growth of algae or decaying matter (like a dead fish) in the water. Spotting it quickly can prevent a rapid die-off of your fish. For this reason, a turbidity sensor in your water can be very helpful.

Figure 9.1 shows a turbidity sensor that can be found on eBay for about $20 or Amazon for about $25.

Figure 9.1

The sensor simply consists of a light source and a light sensor with a gap between them in a clear plastic container. If the water in the gap is cloudy, partially blocks the beam of light between the light and the sensor. You can see the actual sensor at the left of the picture. This has three wires that connect to a circuit board. Three wires then go from the circuit board to the Arduino. One wire goes from the V pin on the circuit board to the Arduino 5V, one to goes from the G pin to the GND pin on the Arduino, and the pin labelled A goes to any Arduino analog input. When the Arduino reads the analog input pin, it gets a higher reading for clear water than cloudy water. In my experiments, it read about 800 on a scale of 0 to 1023, which means it was about 4 volts. When I block it off totally by inserting an opaque object, it reads about 6 out of 1023.

To use the sensor, it needs to be put into the water with the detector down in the water. The top, where the wires go into the sensor, is not waterproof. There is actually a small square hole on the top. Therefore, the top must be kept out of the water. The sensor itself floats, but may tend to tip over so that the hole is in the water. I suggest having it float on the water on a small, thin raft with a hole about 30 mm (1.2 inches) in diameter for the sensor. Since the sensor itself floats, this is just to stop it from tipping over. You can also cover the top with a piece of tape to prevent splashing water from entering the hole. Figure 9.2 shows the top and bottom view of the sensor attached to a small circular raft printed with a 3D printer, as an example. The object infill is set to 10%, so there is a lot of empty space inside the raft to make it float. I have added two small holes, and wrapped a tie strip through the holes and the slot in the sensor to hold the sensor in place. If you do this, be sure to use a very thin wire, thread or piece of fishing line so you do not block the sensor.

Figure 9.2

Since the input reading of the analog input falls as turbidity increases, the Arduino sketch to use this sensor needs to check for low input readings. You can select what level is not acceptable using the serial monitor interface, as has been discussed in previous chapters. Sketch 9.1 does this.

```
#include <EEPROM.h>
#define TActionPin 13
#define TInput A3
int Clear = 400;
unsigned long TurbidityDelay = 600;
int Clarity;
byte HighByte;
byte LowByte;
String CalCommand;
unsigned long PreviousTime = 0;

void setup() {
  Serial.begin(9600);
  pinMode(TActionPin, OUTPUT);
  digitalWrite(TActionPin, LOW);
  HighByte = EEPROM.read(38);
  LowByte = EEPROM.read(39);
  if (HighByte + LowByte < 510) {
     Clear = (HighByte << 8) + LowByte;
  }
  Serial.print("Clear = ");
  Serial.println(Clear);
}

void loop() {
   while (Serial.available()) {
     delay(4);  //delay to allow buffer to fill
     if (Serial.available() >0) {
       char c = Serial.read();
       CalCommand += c;
     }
```

```
  } //End of while loop that reads string
  if (CalCommand.length() >0){
    CalCommand.toUpperCase();
    Serial.println(CalCommand);
    if (CalCommand.startsWith("MC")) {
      CalCommand = CalCommand.substring(2);
      Clear = CalCommand.toInt();
      EEPROM.write(38, highByte(Clear));
      EEPROM.write(39, lowByte(Clear));
      Serial.print("Clear = ");
      Serial.println(Clear);
    }
    if (CalCommand == "S") {
      Clarity = GetMiddleAnalog();
      Serial.print("Clarity = ");
      Serial.println(Clarity);
    }
    CalCommand = "";
  } // End of if (CalCommand.length() >0)
  if (millis() < PreviousTime) {PreviousTime = 0;}
  if (millis() - PreviousTime >= TurbidityDelay * 1000) {
    Clarity = GetMiddleAnalog();
    Serial.println(Clarity);
    if (Clarity < Clear) {
      digitalWrite(TActionPin, HIGH);
      Serial.println("Too turbid");
    }
    else {
      digitalWrite(TActionPin, LOW);
    }
    PreviousTime = millis();
  }
}

unsigned int GetMiddleAnalog(){
  int i, j;
  int n = 5;
  int temp;
```

```
int arr[5];
for (i = 0; i < n; i++){
  arr[i] = analogRead(A3);
  delay(100);
}
for (i = 0; i < n; i++){
  for (j = 0; j < n-1; j++) {
    if (arr[j] > arr[j+1]) {
      int temp = arr[j];
      arr[j] = arr[j+1];
      arr[j+1] = temp;
    }
  }
}
return arr[2];
}// End GetMiddleAnalog
```
Sketch 9.1

Like some previous sketches, this takes readings and sends them to the serial monitor. It is set to take a reading once every ten minutes, but you can force it to send a reading by sending the letter S from the serial monitor. Since the readings go up as water clarity improves, I refer to the readings as clarity levels rather than turbidity levels to make it more intuitive. You can set the minimum acceptable clarity level by sending the command MC### (MC stands for Minimal Clarity), where ### is a number for an analog input reading. You can select this trigger point in two ways. You can put the probe in the tank when the water clarity is at an acceptable level, send the S command several times, and observe the lowest level the reading give, then pick an arbitrary point below this. For example, if you observe that the readings are running between 750 and 760 (some fluctuations are to be expected), you can type MC600 to set the trigger point at 600. You can also take a water sample that is of acceptable quality, insert the probe, and then slowly add some harmless liquid (I used V-8 juice in my experiments) to the water until it reaches a level of cloudiness that you would find unacceptable. Then send the S command, check the readings and input that value.

In Sketch 9.1, the EEPROM file is included to allow you to save the value. Action pin is set to digital output 13 and the analog input is set to A3. These are, as usual, arbitrary selections that you can change. The variable Clear holds the minimal acceptable level of clarity, and a default value of 400 is set. This is an arbitrary value I have selected, and it will be the value until you input a new one. If you are typing the sketch, be sure to start Clear with capital C, or it will conflict with the reserved word clear.

TurbidityDelay is the delay between readings in seconds. I have set it to 600 seconds, which is ten minutes. Clarity is the current reading, and the other variables are as used in previous sketches.

The setup routine initialized serial communications, configures the action output pin, and reads in the stored value of the Clear setting. If no setting has been stored, the memory locations 38 and 39 will each have the default value of 255, the sum will be 510, and the value will not be stored in Clear.

In the loop routine, it starts out with the same type of serial input we have seen in previous chapters. In this case, it responds to the commands MC### and S. When you use the MC### command, it converts the ### in the command to an integer with the line
Clear = CalCommand.toInt();
The next to lines then store the number in memory locations 38 and 39. The Serial.print and Serial.println lines echo the value back to you to confirm that the correct number has been stored.

The line
if (millis() < PreviousTime) {PreviousTime = 0;}
checks for millis() rollover, as in previous chapters. The line
if (millis() - PreviousTime >= TurbidityDelay * 1000) {

checks to see if the time since the last test is equal to or greater than the TurbidityDelay setting. If so, the next line gets the middle analog reading from the GetMiddleAnalog() subroutine and stores it in the Clarity variable. Then, the code checks to see if the Clarity reading is lower than the Clear limit. If the reading is too low, the statement

digitalWrite(TActionPin, HIGH);

turns on the action pin. This can turn on a filter to filter out whatever is in the water, or just an alarm or indicator light. The else statement turns off this device by setting the TActionPin pin LOW when the Clarity is no longer too low. After this test, the statement

PreviousTime = millis();

resets the start of the timer to the present time.

    The GetMiddleAnalog() subroutine works like in previous chapters. It returns the middle value of five analog readings. This prevents a sudden spike caused by a small particle or other obstruction drifting through the sensor.

Chapter 10

Displaying data on screen

In previous chapters, I have used the Serial.print command to have the Arduino send actual numbers such as pH to the serial monitor. You can also display the data on an LCD display connected to your Arduino. While these displays may not be able to display as much data as the serial monitor, and you cannot use them to send data back to the Arduino such as the calibration commands, they are more convenient than connecting a computer to the Arduino for routine readings.

There are several types of LCD display. One type connects to GND and digital pins 2, 3, 4, 5, 11, and 12. The other type, called an I2C display, connects to the SDA and SCL pins. I recommend the I2C LCD display, and will use that in this book. The back of an I2C LCD has four connection pins as shown in Figure 10.1.

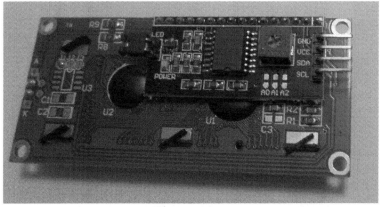

Figure 10.1

You would use the same type of female-male cables you used to connect many of the sensors in previous chapters. The GND pin goes to the Arduino GND and the VCC pin goes to the Arduino 5V. On the Uno, the display's SDA pin goes to the Arduino analog A4 connection and the SCL pin connects to the A5 connection. On the Mega, the SDA connects to pin 20 and the SCL to pin 21.

You need the Wire library to use this display, but that comes installed in the Arduino IDE, so you do not need to download it. You will also need the LCD library Arduino-LiquidCrystal-I2C-library. You can use the Library Manager as described in Chapter 1. You can put I2C in the filter box to narrow the search and then select to install Arduino-LiquidCrystal-I2C-library-master. If you prefer to use the download ZIP file technique, you can download the ZIP file from
https://github.com/fdebrabander/Arduino-LiquidCrystal-I2C-library

In order to use the LCD your sketch, you need the lines
#include <Wire.h>
#include <LiquidCrystal_I2C.h>

You also need to follow these with a line like
LiquidCrystal_I2C lcd(0x27, 20, 4);
The three numbers will vary depending on exactly which LCD display you use. First, there are two sizes. One has 20 characters and 4 lines. The other has 16 characters and 2 lines. Obviously, the 20 by 4 display is more useful and only costs about $2.00 more. However, if you are using the 16 by 2 display, replace the "20, 4" in the above line with "16, 2". The trickier part is the first number, the 0x27 in the example line above. This is the I2C address, and varies with the manufacturer of the display. It is usually 0x27 or 0x3F, although it can be 0x20 if there has been some rewiring done. If none of these work, you can find the I2C address with the scanner software given in Sketch 10.1.

#include <Wire.h>
byte error, address;
int nDevices;

```
void setup(){
  Wire.begin();
  Serial.begin(9600);
  Serial.println("Scanning for I2C addresses");
  nDevices = 0;
  for(address = 1; address < 127; address++ ){
    Wire.beginTransmission(address);
    error = Wire.endTransmission();
    if (error == 0){
      Serial.print("I2C device found at address 0x");
      if (address<16){Serial.print("0");}
      Serial.println(address,HEX);
      nDevices++;
    }
    else if (error==4){
      Serial.print("Unknown error at address 0x");
      if (address<16){Serial.print("0");}
      Serial.println(address,HEX);
    }
  }
  if (nDevices == 0)
    Serial.println("No I2C devices found");
  else
    Serial.println("done");
}

void loop(){
}
```

Sketch 10.1

When you run this sketch, it checks every possible I2C address to see if it exists. It then lists all addresses found on the serial monitor. If you connect the LCD display (and only the LCD display) to the Arduino and run this sketch, the address given should be the I2C address of your display. Just copy this address into the

LiquidCrystal_I2C lcd command as the first parameter. I will not go into explaining this sketch, because you have no need to modify it.

In the setup routine, you need to add
lcd.begin();
You can also add the command
lcd.backlight();
This turns on the backlight, although usually you do not need this because the backlight is usually on by default.

To actually write to the display, you first need to specify the position with the command
lcd.setCursor(X,Y);
where X and Y are the column and row to position the cursor. For example,
lcd.setCursor(2,0);
sets the position of the next write to the third column in the first row. This is because the column and row numbers start with 0, not 1. The command
lcd.setCursor(0,0);
sets the print position to the upper left corner of the display, the normal starting point.

Once you have set the position, the command
lcd.print("text");
prints text. You do need to enclose text you want to print in quotation marks. If you leave out the quotation marks, you can print numeric values. For example,
lcd.print(V);
displays the value of V, which must have been set by your sketch before the print command. The print command leaves the cursor at the end of the text or value last printed, so the sequence of commands
lcd.print("A0 = ");
lcd.print(A0Value);
prints "A0 = 1000", assuming that the variable A0Value has a value of 1000.

Sketch 10.2 demonstrates these principles by displaying the values of the analog inputs A0 and A1.

```
#include <Wire.h>
#include <LiquidCrystal_I2C.h>

// set the LCD address to 0x27 with 20 chars and 4 lines
LiquidCrystal_I2C lcd(0x27,20,4);
int A0V;
int A1V;

void setup(){
  lcd.begin();
  lcd.backlight();
}// End setup

void loop() {
  A0V = analogRead(A0);
  A1V = analogRead(A1);
  lcd.setCursor(0,0); //Set position
  lcd.print("                    "); //Clear the line on the LCD
  lcd.setCursor(0,0); //Set position
  lcd.print("A0 = ");
  lcd.print(A0V);
  lcd.setCursor(0,1); //Set position
  lcd.print("                    "); //Clear the line on the LCD
  lcd.setCursor(0,1); //Set position
  lcd.print("A1 = ");
  lcd.print(A1V);
  delay(1000);
} // End main loop
```

Sketch 10.2

The loop command reads the analog inputs and stores the values in A0V and A1V. It then sets the position to the upper left corner of the screen. It then clears the line by printing 20 spaces. (Make that 16 if you are using a 2 by 16 character display.) This is necessary because the lcd.print command overwrites whatever was in that position before, but does not clear the rest of the line. If you do not clear the line, you may have residue from the previous print. For example, if the previous line was 12345 and the new line is abcd, the line will read abcd5. You do not need to clear the line if you are absolutely sure that the new line will be the same length or longer than the previous line, but you are rarely sure of that when displaying numeric values.

The code then repositions the cursor at the beginning of the line and prints "A0 = ". It then prints the value of A0V at the current position. It then repeats this for A1V. It delays 1000 milliseconds (one second), and the loop repeats. Figure 10.2 shows this in action.

Figure 10.2

In the programs from the previous chapters, you can replace the Serial.print commands with lcd.print. Bear in mind that there are some differences. You have only two or four lines, so you cannot display as much information as the serial monitor. You also need to position your output before you print. While the Serial.println command automatically moves you to the next line, the lcd.print command leaves the cursor in the current position. Also, you usually need to clear the line of previous text. Thus,
Serial.print("A0 = ");
Serial.println(A0V);
Serial.print("A1 = ");
Serial.println(A1V);

can be replaced by the code

```
lcd.setCursor(0,0); //Set position
lcd.print("                    "); //Clear the line on the LCD
lcd.setCursor(0,0); //Set position
lcd.print("A0 = ");
lcd.print(A0V);
lcd.setCursor(0,1); //Set position
lcd.print("                    "); //Clear the line on the LCD
lcd.setCursor(0,1); //Set position
lcd.print("A1 = ");
lcd.print(A1V);
```

A simple practical example would be the EC meter calibration from Chapter 8, Sketch 8.1. In that sketch, you wanted to see frequent displays of the EC readings so that you could turn the calibration screw. Having a small display could be more convenient than hooking the Arduino to the computer. Sketch 10.3 is Sketch 8.1 with the Serial.print statements replaced with the appropriate lcd display statements.

```
#include <LiquidCrystal_I2C.h>

// set the LCD address to 0x27 with 20 chars and 4 lines
LiquidCrystal_I2C lcd(0x27,20,4);

const int Probe = 500;
const int Convert = 250; // or 320 or 350
int A0V;
unsigned int EC;
unsigned int PPM;

void setup(){
  lcd.begin();
  lcd.backlight();
}// End setup

void loop() {
```

```
A0V = analogRead(A0);
EC = map(A0V, 0, 1023, 0, Probe);
PPM = map(A0V, 0, 1023, 0, Convert);
lcd.setCursor(0,0);
lcd.print("                ");
lcd.setCursor(0,0);
lcd.print("A0 = ");
lcd.print(A0V);
lcd.print(" = ");
lcd.print((A0V/1023.0)*5);
lcd.print(" V");
lcd.setCursor(0,1);
lcd.print("                ");
lcd.setCursor(0,1);
lcd.print("EC = ");
lcd.print(EC);
lcd.setCursor(0,2);
lcd.print("                ");
lcd.setCursor(0,2);
lcd.print("TDS = ");
lcd.print(PPM);
lcd.print(" PPM");
delay(1000);
} // End main loop
```
Sketch 10.3

    If you compare this to Sketch 8.1, one other change you might notice is that I have considerably shortened the delay time. One other advantage of using an LCD screen over using the serial monitor is that you do not have to worry about the text scrolling too fast to read, since the text is displayed in the same place each time. You do still need some delay, however, to give the screen time to display the data. If the delay is too short, the display will flicker as data is rapidly written and rewritten.

Chapter 11

Displaying Data on a Web page

You may want to have the readings collected by the Arduino on a Web page so that you can monitor your garden from anywhere. In this chapter, I will discuss setting up a free Web site and displaying data on that side using a program called Serial to Web that I have written and sell.

Serial to Web is a Windows program that will automatically post any text that comes in a serial port of your computer to a Web page. It inputs the information that comes in the serial com port just like the Arduino serial monitor does. It then builds a Web page using the text that it receives and uploads the Web page to a Web host using FTP. The great thing is that there are many hosts that allow you to post Web pages, and some of them are absolutely free. I will provide information on some of these free Web hosts in this chapter, so you can quickly start posting your Arduino data for free. Well, almost free. Serial to Web has a one-time purchase price of $20.00. This is for a license to use Serial to Web on one computer indefinitely. Serial to Web is distributed as shareware. You can download it, install it on your computer, and use it free for 30 days before paying anything to make sure that it is working properly. At the end of the 30-day free trial, it will shut down until you input a registration code that you get when you purchase the program.

Serial to Web is extremely easy to use. Just install it on your computer, fill in some text boxes with information about your Web host and the properties you want for your website, plug your Arduino into the USB port, select your com port (which Serial to Web helps you do), and click on the Run box. Your data will start posting as soon as it comes in from the Arduino.

Hosting sites

Before we get into how to use Serial to Web, you need a little information on Web hosts. In order to post your data, you will need to have a Web host that allows you to upload files by FTP. There are many services that allow you to host Web sites. Some charge you an annual or monthly fee, some are free. Of course, the free ones will then try to encourage you to upgrade to premium services that they charge monthly fees for. The premium plans usually allow you to post more and larger files, allow you to upload and download more bytes per month, and may provide some additional benefits like tech support. However, for uploading just a small file of a few hundred bytes displaying a list of data, the free plan should be sufficient, unless you upload and download the file VERY often.

Here are some free hosting sites that I have found work well with Serial to Web. Each of these allows you to create a site that has a name appended onto their Web address. In the examples below, YourName is the name that you pick for your site and YourUserName is the user name you pick. You will be asked to select a password for your account. This same password will be your FTP file transfer password. You will create a user name for your account. You will also have a user name for FPT file transfers. Some of these use the user name you picked for your account, and some generate a random name.

Pro Free Host
Web site: https://profreehost.com/
Your site: YourName.unaux.com
FTP user name: randomly generated by Pro Free host. A typical FTP user name might be unaux_20428347
FTP upload URL: ftp.unaux.com

000webhost
Web site: https://www.000webhost.com/
Your site: YourUserName.000webhostapp.com
FTP user name: Chosen by you
FTP upload URL: files.000webhost.com

Byet
Web site: https://byet.host/
Your site: YourName.byethost##.com, where ## is a number assigned by Byet
FTP user name: randomly generated by Pro Free host, such as b10_20400914
FTP upload URL: ftp.byethost##.com, where ## is the same number as your Web site

Please be aware that free hosting sites are a somewhat unstable business. Any information given here is as of the time this book is published. Any Web hosts described here may change their business practices, or even go out of business entirely after a while. This is why I have provided information on three different Web hosts. If one or even two of these eventually go out of business, you will still have at least one to use. Of course, you can always find additional free Web host companies by doing a Google search for something like Free Web Hosting. Since you will need a Web hosting company that allows FTP uploads of Web pages, you might want to search for Free Web Hosting FTP. Just be sure that the Web host does allow FTP uploads before you spend too much time getting signed up with the host.

Of course, if you are willing to shell out a few dollars per month to maintain your site, you can go with a paid site like Blue Host or GoDaddy. I will not go into any detail on these as I have with the free sites, since they provide more technical support and you are better off getting direct help from them to suit your individual needs.

Obtaining and installing Serial to Web

Once you have a Web server to upload to, you need to download and install Serial to Web. Serial to Web can be downloaded from Leithauser Research. The general Web page is https://LeithauserResearch.com/, and you can scroll down to near the bottom to find the link to the specific page, but you can go directly to the specific Web page for Serial to Web at https://LeithauserResearch.com/s2w.html

On that page, click on the Click here link in the sentence that says "Click here to download the installation program (s2warc.exe) as a self-extracting file." If your Web browser gives you the option to run it, you can do so. If you download the file, you will need to run it. However, Windows 10 may require that the program be run as administrator because the install program installs files in areas of Windows that require administrator permission. This means you need to right click on the file with your mouse and select "Run as administrator" from the menu that drops down. If you do not run it as administrator, you may get a message like "The requested operation requires elevation." Once the install program is running, you will probably also get messages asking you if the program has permission to make changes to your computer. You must, of course, answer yes.

Once the program is installed, the Serial to Web icon will appear on your desktop. It looks like five computers connected together. Just double click on this to run Serial to Web.

Once you run the program, you will have a 30-day free trial to see if you like it. A registration screen will pop up each time you run the program. At the end of the 30-day free trial, the program will stop working until you pay for it and input the registration code that you will get when you pay for the program. The price is $20.00. This is a onetime fee that allows you to use Serial to Web on one computer indefinitely. More information on purchasing the Serial to Web registration code is provided at the end of this chapter.

Using Serial to Web

Once installed Serial to Web, you first need to configure it for your Web hosting service. When you first run the program, you should see a screen something like Figure 11.1.

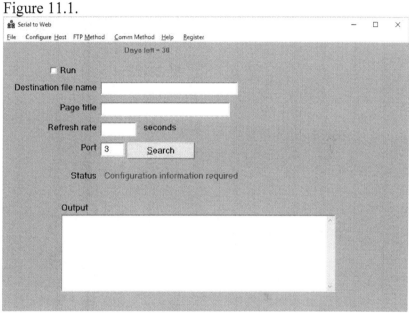

Figure 11.1

Click on the Configure Host menu at the top of the screen. You should then see a screen like Figure 11.2.

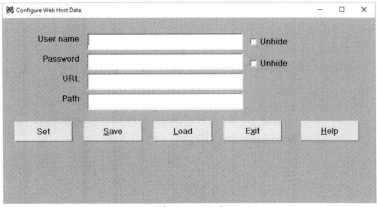

Figure 11.2

There are text boxes for four pieces of information that you need to provide.

You must input the FTP user name and password of your account. As explained in the section of this document on hosting sites, the password is chosen by you and the user name is either chosen by you or generated by the host. Note that by default, these are masked out on the Serial to Web configuration screen for security. Each character is replaced by an asterisk. However, if you check the boxes next to each of these two text boxes, you will be able to see what you are typing.

You must provide the ftp URL of your host, which will be provided by your host site provider, as described in the section of this chapter on hosting sites. You must also provide the path within this FTP URL that you are supposed to upload to. To name a few examples, for files.000webhost.com the path is /public_html/. For both Byet and Pro Free Host, it is /htdocs/. For Blue Host it is /public_html/YourSite/, where YourSite is the name of your site without the extension. For example, if your site is ArduionoData.com, the path would be /public_html/ArduionoData /. Regardless of which host you use, the path you input into the Serial to Web configuration screen must begin and end with a forward slash (/). The path must be at least a forward slash (/), even if your host does not require a path.

Unfortunately, the proper path is one thing that the hosting companies are not usually very diligent in providing. One way to determine this is to open Windows Explorer on your computer and input the ftp address for the site in the format ftp://ftpsite.com, where ftpsite.com is the FTP URL. Windows Explorer should then ask you for your user name and password. Once you input these, you should see a folder display that looks much like the folders on your computer. From this, you should be able to figure out which folder to upload to. In many cases, there will actually be messages in the folder saying "Do not upload to this folder" and "Upload your files here."

There are several buttons below the text boxes on the configuration screen. The Set button sets the information as your current information and will be used to transmit the data from your serial port. The Save button saves the information into a file. When you press the Save button, a text box and Ok button will appear. The text box is for the name of the file to save the information in. By default, this box will be filled with the FTP URL, minus the extension (like .com) and the prefix (like www or ftp). If you are satisfied with the name, click on the Ok button to save the information to this file. Note that the Save button does not set the information as your current information. If you exit the configuration screen without clicking on the Set button, the program will not be set to use this information. Likewise, clicking on the Set button does not save the information to disk. If you do not click on the Save button, the information will be lost when you shut down Serial to Web.

The load button will load a previously saved file. If you click on this button, a drop down box will appear. Click on the down arrow at the right of this box to display a list of files you have saved. Click on the name of the file you want to load. Note that you will only need this option if you have multiple Web hosts and you want to switch between hosts. Once you have saved information, the most recently saved information will automatically be loaded with Serial to Web runs. If you have only one hosted Web site, you will never need to go back to the Configure Web Host Data screen again.

The Exit button closes the Configure Web Host Data screen and returns you to the main screen. If you attempt to exit when you have changed any data but not set or saved that data, the program will display a warning screen and ask if you want to continue to exit. The normal answer in this case would be No. You should normally both set and save any changes you have made to the data before you exit the configure screen.

Back at the main screen, there is additional information to input. You will need to input a destination file name, the name the file will have on the hosting server. If you want your Web site to display the data page as the default page, you should generally name it index.html. If you want to have a different main page and have a link to the data page, you should give it another name, such as data.html.

You can also provide a page title. This is optional, but the page title is displayed on search engines and at the top of some web browsers, so it helps identify your page.

The refresh rate is how often you want the web page (in seconds) to automatically reload in the viewer's Web browser. If you leave this box empty or input 0, the page will not automatically refresh itself. Unless you really need to watch a frequently changing display, it is often best to not have the page refresh. For one thing, some hosting sites charge you based on data transfer, and having the page refresh itself over and over causes it to transfer data. Some of the free hosting sites limit the number of transfers you can have per month. There is one other matter you need to know about having the page automatically refresh. If you are having new pages sent to your site frequently, there is a chance that your Web browser will try to download the page just as the new page is uploading. This can cause the download to fail, and you to suddenly have a blank screen. If this happens, you have no Web page loaded and the refreshing will stop, because the refresh command is actually on the Web page. If this happens, just hit the refresh button on your Web browser to load the page and restart the process.

The port that the main Serial to Web page is asking for is which serial port you want to accept data from. When you connect your Arduino or other device to the USB port, it is automatically assigned a port number. Usually, the newest device plugged into the USB port will have the highest number. When you run Serial to Web, it automatically scans the ports and makes a list of all ports in use. It then puts the highest port number into this text box. If you plugged an Arduino into the USB port before you ran Serial to Web, the port number shown in the box has a very good chance of being the one connected to the Arduino. If you did not have the Arduino connected before you ran Serial to Web, you can connect it and then click on the Search button. This will cause Serial to Web to rescan the ports and put the highest number in the box again. If you find that you are not getting input from the Arduino when you start the upload process (discussed shortly), you can open the Arduino IDE and check under the Tools menu to see which port the Arduino is connected to, then manually put that port number into the box. Note that even if you do not have an Arduino connected to the computer, there may be other serial ports on your computer, so this text box may have a value in it when you run Serial to Web despite you not having an Arduino connected.

There are two other settings on the Serial to Web main screen. At the top of the screen, you will see a menu item that says "FTP Method" and one that says "Comm Method." If you click on either of these, you will see a dropdown menu that lists Method 1 and Method 2. The FTP methods are two methods of transmitting the file by FTP. The Comm methods are methods for reading data from the Arduino serial port. Method 1 is checked by default on each of these. You probably will never need to concern yourself with these. Method 1 normally works best for both. However, in the very unlikely event that there is some problem with this method for either of these on your system, you can switch to method 2 to see if that works better. If the comm method is not working, you will never see information displayed in the output text box (explained below). If the FTP method is not working, you may see a message displayed saying that the data was transmitted but not see the data on your Web page. Again, these situations are unlikely, but alternate methods are provided in case there is any incompatibility with your system.

Once you have plugged in your Arduino and supplied all the above information, Serial to Web is ready to go. To start uploading data from the serial port, just check the Run box. (Click on it again to uncheck it and stop the uploading.) Serial to Web will check the serial port once every .5 seconds. It will store the input. When it receives the transmit code, which is @@@@ (four @ symbols in a row), from the Arduino, it will convert the text received so far into a Web page and then send that Web page to your site by FTP. (I will cover this in the following section on programming the Arduino.) To stop uploading, just uncheck the Run button by clicking on it again.

There is a box at the bottom of the screen that shows what is being received from the Arduino. It should look pretty much like what your Web page will look like, although it does not interpret any html code you have the Arduino insert into the message. (More on that in the following section.)

Fire Walls

If you have a firewall on your computer, it is quite likely that your computer firewall will try to block Serial to Web from sending the Web page. If you have Windows Defender, it will display a small window asking you if you want to allow this application to access the Internet. Just click on the button to allow this. You will only have to do this once, and Windows Defender will always allow transmissions from Serial to Web. If you are using MacAfee, the problem is more serious. MacAfee has settings that are supposed to make it ask you if you want to block any program that tries to access the Internet, but I could not get these to work in my tests. I found that the only way to allow Serial to Web to work was to turn off the firewall totally with MacAfee. I have had other problems with MacAfee in the past, and do not recommend it. Other firewalls may present other difficulties.

Note: If your firewall blocks Serial to Web for too long, Serial to Web may lock up and need to be shut down and restarted. It is therefore important to respond immediately to any request from your firewall for permission to allow access to the Internet by Serial to Web. Another tip is to exit Serial to Web with File/Exit after you have input all configuration information and restart it before the first time you click on the Run box. This will ensure that Serial to Web has saved all information in case you have to force a shutdown of Serial to Web.

Programming the Arduino

I assume that by now you are familiar enough with the Arduino to do the basic programming for whatever your project is, and just need to know how to format the output to Serial to Web. It is just a simple matter of using the Serial.print and Serial.println commands. Below is a simple Arduino sketch that outputs the reading from three analog ports of an Arduino Uno once every ten seconds.

```
void setup() {
  Serial.begin(9600);
}

void loop() {
```

```
  Serial.print("A0 = ");
  Serial.println(analogRead(A0));
  Serial.print("A1 = ");
  Serial.println(analogRead(A1));
  Serial.print("A2 = ");
  Serial.println(analogRead(A2));
  Serial.print("@@@@");
  delay(10000);
}
```

This sketch opens the serial port in the setup routine. In the loop routine, it prints "A0 =" and then prints the value of A0. Note that it uses Serial.println to print the value, so there is a line feed. On the serial monitor, this would cause it to go to the next line. The Serial to Web program will insert a <br>, which is html code for a line feed, into the Web page every time it receives a line feed from the Arduino. This will cause the Web page to look like the display of the serial monitor. Thus, you can write the Arduino code to display on the Web page exactly as you would write it to display on the serial monitor.

The sketch then does the same thing for the other two values of the analog inputs. Then the sketch sends the @@@@ to the serial port. This is the signal for Serial to Web that it is the end of the message to be sent to the Web page.

After sending the @@@@ signal, this sketch delays ten seconds and then sends the readings again. This is just an arbitrary time that causes the readings to be sent every 10 seconds, and you can set the delay to be anything you want as long as it allows Serial to Web to create the Web page and transmit it by FTP (usually a few seconds). In fact, an even better system is to resend the information when it changes, not at a set interval. The next sketch sends the readings when any of them change.

```
int Reading1;
int Reading2;
int Reading3;
int PreviousReading1;
int PreviousReading2;
int PreviousReading3;

void setup() {
  Serial.begin(9600);
}

void loop() {
  PreviousReading1 = Reading1;
  PreviousReading2 = Reading2;
  PreviousReading3 = Reading3;
  Reading1 = analogRead(A0);
  Reading2 = analogRead(A1);
  Reading3 = analogRead(A2);
  if (PreviousReading1 != Reading1 || PreviousReading2 != Reading2 || PreviousReading3 != Reading3) {
    Serial.print("A0 = ");
    Serial.println(Reading1);
    Serial.print("A1 = ");
    Serial.println(Reading2);
    Serial.print("A2 = ");
    Serial.println(Reading3);
    Serial.print("@@@@");
    delay(5000);
  }
}
```

This sketch saves the readings in the PreviousReading# before it stores a new reading in Reading#. It then compares the previous readings with the new ones. If the first one or the second one or the third one is not equal, it transmits the readings. It then sends the @@@@ end of message signal. It then delays 5 seconds to allow Serial to Web to finish uploading the file before it tests again, just so that Serial to Web does not get backed up.

You can even do some simple bar graphs by adding code like this.

```
for (int i = 0; i < Reading1/10; i++){
    Serial.print("=");
}
Serial.println();
```

If you are familiar with html code, or even other code like JavaScript, you can have the Arduino print such code into the message. For example, you can make part of the text bigger with lines like

```
Serial.print("<h1>");
Serial.print("Whatever you want to print");
Serial.print("</h1>");
```

I want to stress that these examples are for illustration purposes. You can have the Arduino send any message you want displayed on your Web page, followed by the @@@@ send message signal.

You should be aware that each serial port can only be connected to one device at a time. While Serial to Web is running and linked to the port (which happens when you check the Run box), you cannot download a new sketch to your Arduino. If you want to update your Arduino sketch, you must exit from Serial to Web. The best way to do this is to click on File and then Exit.

Purchasing Serial to Web

Serial to Web is distributed as shareware. Once you download it and install it on your computer, you can try it free for 30 days. During this time, it will display a registration screen each time you run it, and also if you click on the Register menu at the top right of the screen. There is a text box on this registration screen where you can input a registration code. At the end of the free trial period, Serial to Web will become disabled until you input the registration code, which you can purchase for $20, into the text box on the registration screen and click the Ok button. Once you have input the registration code, Serial to Web will operate indefinitely. The purchase price is a one-time fee. If you do not yet have the registration code but have time left in your trial period, click on the Ok button to close the registration screen and continue using Serial to Web.

You can purchase the registration code through PayPal by going to LeithauserResearch.com and clicking on the pictures of credit cards, or going directly to https://leithauserresearch.com/paylr.html. Once on this page, scroll down to Serial to Web on the payment page, input the serial number displayed on the Serial to Web registration screen second line, and then click on the Buy Now button. You can also call Leithauser Research at 386-738-0418 between the hours of 10 AM and 10 PM Eastern time to charge your credit card over the phone. You can also send a check for $20.00 to

Leithauser Research
3624 Royal Fern Circle
Deland, FL 32724

Be sure to include the serial number displayed on the registration screen in your cover letter, along with an email address or phone number (preferably both in case one is hard to read) where you can be reached to give you the registration code.

If you have any questions, you can send them to Leithauser@aol.com.

Chapter 12

More Ideas and Information

There are lots of possible additions and improvements you can make in the materials discussed in this book. I hope that I have explained the sketches clearly enough for you to build on what I have written. In this chapter, I will try to give you some ideas.

One idea that can be useful is to connect the Arduinos by radio, using pair of nRF24L01 radio transceivers. You can buy a pair of long range nRF24L01 transceivers on Amazon.com or eBay. The nRF24L01 comes in two versions: a small short range (about 100 meters, 328 feet) version and a longer range (about 1 kilometer, .6 miles) that has a range extending antenna. Note that ranges are for line-of-sight with no obstacles. This would allow you to have the Arduinos interact without needing to have wires running between them. This can be especially useful when using Serial to Web, because your computer that uploads the text to the Web site can be far from your aquaponics garden. It can also allow you to have the LCD screen that displays information be in your house or other more convenient location than in your garden.

I have written a book about how to connect Arduinos using the nRF24L01 entitled "Remote Sensor Monitoring by Radio with Arduino: Detecting Intruders, Fires, Flammable and Toxic Gases, and Other Hazards at a Distance." This book is available on Amazon.com on Kindle ($4.99) or as paperback ($9.99). I had originally intended to include much of the information from that book in this one because it could be useful. However, I realized that including a fairly large portion of that book within this one would vastly increase the size, and therefore the cost, of this book. Since it might be unfair to some people who are not interested in linking their Arduinos to add so much cost to this book, I will simply refer you to that book for people who want to do this. Incidentally, that book does include a chapter on detecting power failures that might be of interest to people with remote aquaponics or hydroponic systems.

A similar idea would be to network the Arduinos using Wi-Fi. This could allow you to have Arduinos send emails to you or otherwise alter you if the Arduino detected dangerous readings. Again, I had planned to include such information in this book, but again I realized that it would vastly increase the size of this book with material not directly related to aquaponic or hydroponic gardens, and it is probably better to allow you to get this information from other available books if you are interested.

I have mentioned that you can have the Arduino do more than one type of test. In fact, you could have just one Arduino run all the tests. This not only saves you the cost of multiple Arduinos, it makes it easy to have the tests interact. I have discussed in previous chapters a few examples of having data interact, such as having the conductivity readings adjusted for water temperature or having the timer adjust for air temperature and humidity. You can go further depending on your setup, allowing air temperature to interact with soil moisture readings, turbidity readings to interact with total dissolved solids readings (if both are rising, it could indicate a different situation than if just one is), etc. You can put many functions inside the loop routine, and have them all executed, one after the other. There are a few things you need to bear in mind.

One thing to be careful of is that you do not use the same variable names for different functions. For example, if you have several functions that have upper and lower trigger values, be sure not to call them all UpperLimit and LowerLimit or TooHigh and TooLow. You need to and something to the variable names to distinguish them, like AirTempTooHigh and WaterTempTooLow, and so on. Also, some of the sketches have included delays, such as

Sketch 3.1 and 4.1. Each of these has a delay at the end of the main loop. If you do have this type of delay in several of the sketches you combine, you do not need to include all of the delays, just the longest one.

There may very well be other aspects of your system that you want to monitor. I know, for example, that it would be very useful to monitor ammonia in your fish tank. Unfortunately, this book is limited to sensors that are available at reasonable prices and can be interfaced with Arduinos. I have tried but been unable to find any ammonia sensor that can be connected to an Arduino. Note: If you really want to monitor ammonia, go to https://www.seneye.com/devices for a product that monitors ammonia, pH, and temperature. This does not appear to be compatible with Arduino or actual automation, however, just monitoring.

I believe that if you find any additional sensors that would be useful to you, you can easily adapt the sketches in this book to those sensors. They probably output an analog signal from 0 to 5 volts that you can connect to one of the Arduino analog inputs. Once you have done this, you can easily use most of the sketches in this book that trigger a relay and/or send serial port message for that sensor. Typical examples are sketches 6.1, 6.2, and 9.1 After all, these are simply triggering a relay in response to a certain level at the analog input, and it does not really matter to the sketch what physical parameter determines the voltage input. If they output a digital on-off signal, you can use sketches like 5.3.

To save you the trouble of typing these long sketches, I have uploaded a ZIP file containing the sketches to the following location.
https://github.com/DavidLeithauser/Aquaponic-Automation
This is a public download site of files. At this Web page, click on the "Clone or download" button and then click on "Download ZIP"

I have also uploaded the Zip file with the name AquaponicAutomation.zip to my Leithauser Research company Web site, https://LeithauserResearch.com/
You can download it by typing
https://LeithauserResearch.com/AquaponicAutomation.zip
in your Web browser. This Web site is paid up through February of 2020. I cannot guarantee that I will maintain this Web site beyond that date.

If I post the code to other Web sites in the future, I will attempt to add them to the description of this book on Amazon.com.

Once you have downloaded the ZIP file, extract it. Most Windows computers will automatically extract a ZIP file if you right click on the file name and then click on "extract here." This will create a folder named "AquaponicAutomation." Inside this folder is another folder labeled "examples." Inside this folder are separate folders containing each of the files. The files in this archive have names in the format S#P#, which stands for Sketch # Point #. These names reference the sketch number in this book. For example, a file called S3P1 would be Sketch 3.1 in the book. Copy or move the AquaponicsAutomation folder to your Arduino folder in your Documents folder, and it should show up in Sketchbook under the Arduino File menu. You may need to shut down and restart the IDE if it was running when you added the AquaponicsAutomation folder to the Documents/Arduino folder.

If you have any comments or questions about this book, you can contact me at Leithauser@aol.com.

Made in the USA
San Bernardino,
CA